Sylvia

LIFE IN TUDOR AND STUART TIMES

TIMESPAN is a resource based history course for the new curriculum in primary and middle schools. It covers attainment targets for Key Stages 1 and 2 and the first year of key stage 3.

TIMESPAN aims to provide ideas for the four main areas of resource materials required for inclusion in the curriculum - artefacts, documentary evidence, pictures and stories. Each main area is covered separately.

CLASSROOM SERIES

Each book helps the teacher to identify, organise, classify, describe and use a range of objects in the classroom. Each book also acts as a resource facility when taking children out on educational visits.

Classroom Museum   isbn 1 85450 001 5
A teachers' guide to artefacts in which 100 essential examples are described or illustrated
Classroom Gallery   isbn 1 85450 003 1
A colourful selection of narrative and descriptive pictures from every age, dating from cave-paintings to moon-walking
Classroom Archives   isbn 1 85450 002 3
An expansion on the theme of documents for younger children, with about 100 examples

TELL TALE

An anthology of additional history stories for every study unit. Each will include original sources, documents, pictures and poems. Each Tell Tale covers one unit of the history curriculum and an accompanying folder of pictures is designed to be passed around the class while the story is being told.

No. 1: Invaders & Settlers (Romans, A/Saxons, Vikings) isbn 1 85450 009 0
No. 2: Medieval Realms (1066-1500)   isbn 1 85450 004 X
No. 3: Life in Tudor & Stuart Times (1500-1700)   isbn 0 85450 006 6
No. 4: Victorian Britain   isbn 1 85450 007 4
No. 5: Life in Britain since 1930   isbn 1 85450 011 2

Series Editor: John West
issn 0958 − 7650

TELLTALE THREE

LIFE IN TUDOR AND STUART TIMES

c1500 – c1700

History Stories from Evidence: Resources for the National Curriculum.

JOHN WEST

KEY STAGE TWO

**Each book of TELLTALE corresponds to a British History
Study Unit for the same period.**

1990

This first edition is published August, 1990 by ELM Publications of Seaton House, Kings Ripton, Huntingdon PE17 2NJ (04873-238) and printed by St Edmundsbury Press of Bury St Edmunds, Suffolk.

British Library Cataloguing in Publication Data
West, John
      Tell tale. — (Timespan, ISSN 0958—7650;3)
      Vol. 3, The age of Discovery
      1. History
      I. Title II. Series
      900

      ISBN 1-85450-006-6

LIFE IN TUDOR AND STUART TIMES

CONTENTS

LIFE IN TUDOR AND STUART TIMES

LIST OF ILLUSTRATIONS

BOOK

Denotes maps and diagrams.

LIFE IN TUDOR AND STUART TIMES

LIST OF ILLUSTRATIONS

ACCOMPANYING PACK

Denotes maps and diagrams.

ABOUT THE AUTHOR

John West taught history to primary and secondary school-children before training teachers, advising in Liverpool and Dudley and recently conducting a range of INSET courses. He has researched widely in history at doctorate level on how children learn about the past, and he continues to collect and enjoy Victoriana.

His publications include:-

History 7 - 13: a set of guidelines for teachers

Village Records, Town Records

and several books for school-children.

FOREWORD

STORIES AS EVIDENCE : THE NEW CURRICULUM

The New Curriculum imposes two main requirements upon Primary school History. Firstly, it advocates continual reference to a wide range of original source material, such as artefacts, documents and pictures. Secondly, it recommends the frequent use of stories, to preserve the narrative of History. We must be prepared to make provision for these requirements with children from 8 to 13. Above all, the stories which we tell to children must be suitable for them to ask, with confidence: "Is this story true?" and, with equal confidence enable them to interrogate and test the text. Stories are another aspect of historical evidence.

TELLTALE aims for *knowledge and understanding* in a collection of stories which are firmly based upon original sources. Whether the narrator was a medieval chronicler, a 16th century navigator or a modern newspaper reporter, *TELLTALE* recounts his story - and often hers. Documents too, such as letters, diaries, court rolls and government reports, all these have their own stories to tell. Not all narratives are first-hand, eye-witness accounts; some popular versions of a famous story are not even contemporary with the action. Provided that these second-hand story-tellers have used original sources well, their tales are also told, as secondary evidence. Myths and legends, poems and pictures, all have stories to tell and these too are included.

Every story has been selected for its importance as evidence, often as the official or first-hand account of an event. Some fiction may occasionally seem to be more adventurous than real History, but this is debatable. History stories add the extra excitement of authenticity to adventures which really happened. Many of the stories included are accounts which were contemporary with the action. Others were compiled second-hand, by more or less reliable historians who had access to earlier sources. Some versions of an event will be unreliable hearsay, others give a more objective view.

Recent legal investigations have shown that the infallibility of the eye-witness is a myth. The spectator may have seen less of the game than the more distant observer. Involved in the action, he may have been emotionally shaken, unsighted or biased. Many witnesses see only what they expect to see and recall what they choose to remember. Sometimes a later compiler will have access to more reliable data, a variety of witnesses and the benefits of hindsight. There is, even so, an especial cachet, an air of authority, however spurious, about the proud narrator who claims, from long ago: "I know this, because I was there. I saw it happen!"

Story has been widely interpreted in this collection. Here are, not only chronicles, but also poems and legends; letters and diaries; court-room evidence and official reports. Some of our stories were written by professional historians. From Herodotus, Father of History, the course of History has been regularly charted for the past 2,500 years. In every case it is essential to establish the concept of primary (first-hand) and secondary (second- or hundredfold-hand) sources. The child's own History textbook takes its place at the end of a very long secondary line. So, we always establish the identity, experience and standpoint of each story's Narrator.

TELLTALE does not offer easy texts. Ancient story-tellers like Herodotus, Froissart and the *Daily Mirror* did not, intentionally, write for 8-year-olds; they demand a teacher's interpretation to a class. Very few of our stories could be read by Juniors, though one or two modern versions which were especially written for children are included. Most of the original story-tellers use archaic language and sometimes a ponderous, old-fashioned style. These are features of special value. *TELLTALE* almost always assumes that it is more desirable for stories to be read to children as an attentive audience, than pondered silently, alone.

Each page is, deliberately, uninterrupted by explanatory footnotes or illustrations which would distract the teacher or child from the narrative. All necessary explanations are give in the **Information section** which follows each story, and in a **Glossary** of archaic words. Some of these, the most vivid examples, have been retained to enrich the vocabularies of children who love big words and do not wish to be patronised.

Reading stories is not a simple, off-the-cuff classroom activity; story-telling demands a well-prepared familiarity with the text and continual practice. The teacher must be prepared to use professional skills to read editorially, infusing difficult passages with expression and meaning, substituting easier words if reference to a useful glossary defeats the class, smoothly inserting the occasional explanatory gloss into the narrative. With practice, as most Infant teachers know, this becomes a rewarding experience. Some of the stories, though carefully abridged, are still quite long. These are intended to be read in instalments, lesson by lesson, with interim discussion of each passage. Some passages can be photocopied for individual perusal. Children need more experience of unfamiliar, ancient sources.

To assist the teacher's editorial process, each of *TELLTALE*'s stories has been tried with Primary school children. As a result of their responses the most difficult archaic words have been changed to more familiar forms and longer stories have been carefully abridged, to hold attention. (Sometimes it is impossible to do this without losing the true flavour of the document; in those cases it has been thought better to leave any final changes to the teacher, who might advise us not to under-estimate the children and tamper with the text.) Strange spellings, though these too add to the authenticity of the original text, have been modernised to assist the teacher's reading. They would not, in any case be seen by the children.

Some non-specialist History teachers may find unfamiliar events, people, behaviour and attitudes in some of the stories. *TELLTALE* is about the Attainment Target of *acquiring and evaluating historical information.* Our **Information section** gives the main historical facts, dates and essential knowledge. Illustrations, including story-pictures, maps and portraits, are contained in a separate folder. This teaching material is, in many cases, extensive enough, with the story itself, to introduce and support an entire theme, such as Ships and Seafarers, especially if two or three similar stories from different periods are combined. For some teachers, the **Evidence** and **Information sections,** being factual, may in some lessons take precedence over the more difficult text of the story, which can be used in small portions to enliven the theme and increase the children's understanding of original evidence as the theme develops.

It is not intended that children should accept any story from the past uncritically, just because it is old, or even first-hand evidence. After each narrative section the teacher is offered, as well as the essential background information, a critical analysis of the narrator's viewpoint, experience and, possibly his prejudices. These form a set of questions which **Check the Evidence.** Here, the class is encouraged to challenge the narrator's authority - "How did he know this? What were his sources of information?"; "Was he biased in any way?"; "Did he exaggerate?"; "List the facts he gives. Now list those which he omits"; "Where can we check his facts?"; "Are there other versions of his story?"; "Did the narrator have any special motive in telling his tale? Was he trying to prove something?" These and other questions test the veracity of each story and begin to establish a pattern in the children's approach to any historical account. Each story has its own, more pertinent set of questions; additional, more general suggestions are offered in **Appendix A.** These can be copied and used on cue-cards, to prompt children's group discussion.

It is intended that every story should be capable of association with other verbal and non-verbal relics of its period. Contemporary pictures, museum objects, photographs, documents, even ephemera, confirm or expand the central narrative. Several stories are recounted in two or more versions, including narrative paintings and poems, in order to present conflicting views or corroboration.

In a few cases the reverse is the case; an artefact or picture may lack a story, or a fragment of evidence becomes a mystery. This is inevitable with evidence from prehistoric times or Dark Ages when no written evidence whatever is available. There are even more dubious cases, such as the controversial *Murder of the Princes,* where evidence may have been deliberately suppressed, or perverted for political reasons. In some of these cases (see: *How Robin Hood became an Outlaw in TELLTALE TWO* or: *"And when did you last see your father ...?"* in *TELLTALE THREE* an imaginative story has been woven about a piece of more tangible and evocative evidence. All reconstructions are clearly identified; they offer opportunities for children to practise their skill in detecting and evaluating the "fake" and distinguishing it from reasonably authentic TV style fact-ion.

Our stories also attain the target of *understanding points of view and interpretation.* They inevitably reflect the values of their own age, rather than our own. Some are Jingoistic, even racist in modern terms; too many, like History itself, deal with intolerance, inequalities, conflict and bloodshed. Often, the narrators make it clear that they neither knew nor cared what posterity's judgment might be. Children are encouraged to discuss these problems in the section **"What is your verdict?"** Here teachers should be prepared to guide discussion along two different lines of thought - with reference to both past and present values. The strategies for this approach to the evidence are summarised in **Appendix B**.

In every case we must beware of exchanging our own set of prejudices for an earlier myth. Much of the earlier failings of so-called empathy arose from blatantly egocentric modern prejudice and misunderstanding. The child who believes that Captain Oates was "thick" and not heroic has failed to understand the spirit of 1913. Similarly, a child who finds Froissart's version of Crecy "boring" has watched too much TV and read too little. Those who casually dismiss Lady Butler's war-paintings a "glorifying war" should look at her pictures again. Whilst we must surely ask "What does the story make you feel?", the more important priority is "What did those earlier people feel?"

There must be a place for courage in History - courage against impossible odds, courage in defeat or in face of cruel oppression. In this context, an eight-year-old Black Country nailer was as brave a hero as any soldier, and Douglas Bader was, perhaps, braver when he walked than when he flew. We find heroes in the ranks of exploration, of scientific discovery, as well as on the battle field. Such courage is often lived out quietly and alone, as with Scott in the Antarctic or Mrs. Pankhurst in her prison cell.

Thus we enable our pupils to build up a store of judgment on what we really mean by heroism, élitism, equal opportunities, cruelty, success or wasted effort. Each set of questions, both for **Check the Evidence** and **What is your**

verdict? is variable in its range of difficulty for children in each year of the Key Stages, taking into account the needs of both gifted and so-called less able children. In fact, each set of questions aims to satisfy notional mental ages of 7 to 13. The questions are usually framed in language which is suited to children's understanding, but teachers may feel that the words need rephrasing. Once again it has been thought best to leave the final selection of what best suits a class to their own teacher, who will also bear in mind the Attainment Targets and levels of his age-group's *understanding*.

Simple comprehension questions, about the basic facts of the story, are not included. These are for the individual teacher to devise, wherever necessary, for his/her own class. Most of the maps, diagrams and statistics can usefully be reproduced for classroom use; otherwise they are for the teacher's own information and guidance on the preparation of lessons based on the stories. Most of the language and ideas expressed in this book are intended for transmission to children through the teacher. *TELLTALE*'s assumption, throughout, is that only an individual class-teacher can judge the exact level of suitability of any of this material for his/her class and the individuals in it. The book is a set of guidelines and a basis for the teacher's own lesson preparation.

As children and adults today, we are all engulfed by an inescapable deluge of data - much of it worthless - which pours upon us, almost hourly. In order to understand both present times and past, we need the structure of a story, its beginning, middle and end. We need the moral of a tale, the pride of action, the stimulus of partisan acclaim and the calm of an impartial record. Above all, we must, for our own sakes, learn to distinguish between propaganda and truth, between sentimentality and empathy, heritage and nostalgia.

The fostering of a critical, searching review of our own society's myths cannot be left to chance or political Newspeak. Stories from History offer a source of tried and tested experience in many exciting forms. Sometimes, amongst these, we may find the Truth. Children need more meaningful stories and stories cry out for accomplished story-tellers. Here are a few of the best - and worst - examples of the historian's craft.

John West
Tettenhall : January, 1990

INTRODUCTION: LIFE IN TUDOR AND STUART TIMES
(1500 – 1700)

The History Working Group sets the following requirements for the New Curriculum:

"7.15: Pupils should therefore progress in their ability to gauge the relative reliability and usefulness of a wide range of sources of evidence in seeking historical explanations.   This attainment target (AT3: Acquiring and evaluating historical information) is concerned with the ways in which pupils become involved in history as a process of discovery. It involves experience of different and increasingly complex sources.   Written sources include original documents, books etc. and also the writings of historians." **(Final Report (April 1990) p.116)**.

and:

"10.7: Pupils of all ages will benefit greatly from reading primary sources (or extracts from them), such as diaries, memoirs, broad-sheets, newspapers, poetry and novels dating from the time and place being studied. For example the diary of someone who sailed on a voyage of exploration could make the study of ships and sea-farers vividly memorable. In a different way, reading a Victorian text-book might bring alive the experience of schooling in the nineteenth century. By these means pupils can be encouraged to develop their own individual ideas of similarity and difference, and of continuity and change, between past and present." **(Final Report, (April 1990) p.177)**.

These requirements are met by the *TELLTALE* series, which places each Unit in its historic setting (AT1) by offering first-hand stories as historical evidence (AT3).   Supplementary questions which require pupils to **CHECK THE EVIDENCE** are completely in accordance with hIgh-level attainment of AT3 on acquiring and evaluating historical information.   Those exercises which prompt a **VERDICT** on attitudes and behaviour of past times also demand a confident attainment of AT2 in understanding points of view and interpretations of history – including the pupils' own viewpoint.

Discussion of the stories, interrogation of their narrators, and constructive recording of the pupils' conclusions complete each programme of study in accordance with AT4.

TELLTALE THREE contains a wide range of primary source material for **HSU 3 Key Stage 2: Life in Tudor and Stuart Times**. Essential information, specifically outlined in the programme of study for this Unit, includes original documents and teaching notes on exploration, religious conflict and persecution, especially the development of the printed Bible, Guy Fawkes and the Gunpowder Plot, Armada, 1588, women in action, Drake's circumnavigation of the world, Raleigh's settlement of Virginia, Civil War, Great Plague, 1665 and Fire of London, 1666.

In another term of Key Stage 2, these stories can also be used to supplement **HSU 8: Ships and Seafarers through history**. The stories of Hawkins *(An Elizabethan Pirate)*, Drake *(The World is Round!)*, Raleigh *(A Courtier's Downfall)* and Captain Lechmere *(A Young Sea-Captain)* give a considerable amount of first-hand and reference material, required information about life on board ships, design and decoration of ships, and trade routes and goods from ancient times. The stories bring an otherwise inert Unit to life, supplying opportunities, as the History Working Group recommend: "to demonstrate different interpretations and points of view, for example between the 'romantic' and 'realistic' versions of life aboard sailing ships. (AT2)". **(Final Report p.48)** We have therefore included, not illustrative snippets, not only substantial extracts from Hakluyt's *Principal Voyages* but also from the log-books of Drake's *Golden Hind*, Hawkins's *Jesus*, and Admiral Benbow's squadron in the West Indies.

At a later stage, teachers of **Key Stage 3** can also use these stories, in the Working Group's terms (3.24; 5.23), to 're-visit' the Tudor age and illustrate **HSU 15: The Making of the United Kingdom: c1500-1750**, with particular reference to essential information provided on changes in wealth and power *(The Flower of the North* and *A Courtier's Downfall)* and especially with the use of unusual source material on the era of the Civil War *(Lady Brilliana defends her Castle, The Battle of Naseby, 'And when did you last see your father?'.*

More than mere 'knowledge as information', stories and teaching structures are directly addressed to the attainment of the New Curriculum's specific attainment targets, as follows:-

Attainment Target 1: Understanding history in its setting. The evidence of plotter, pirate, courtier, chatelaine and civil servant present a lifelike historic setting of human motivation **(Level 3)**, cause and consequence **(Level 4)**. As we progress from early religious disorders of Henry VIII's reign to the aggressive nationalism of Elizabethan England, the conflicting loyalties of Cavaliers and Roundheads and the professionalism of sea-captains of the Glorious Revolution's Navy, children cannot fail to gain "a clear understanding of change over varied time periods" and an understanding that "historical events have different types of causes and consequences." **(Level 5)**. With very able children these primary and secondary sources can be directed as high as **Level 7b,** (drawing the distinction between causes, intention, motives and reasons).

Attainment Target 2: Understanding different points of view and interpretations of history. The variety of narrators who tell their tales, from the Tudor Lancaster Herald to Samuel Pepys and from Guy Fawkes to Lady Brilliana Harley, ensures that AT2 is thoroughly covered. The Working Party's **Final Report (pp.127-131)** set their sights fairly low on this target for Primary school children, aiming only at **Levels 2** (Recognise that there can be more than one version of an historical event — as in the Spanish version of the Armada's defeat) to **Level 5** (understand some general reasons why there are different interpretations of historical issues — as in a Puritan lady's view of a Royalist neighbourhood.) As far as *TELLTALE* is concerned, this attainment goes without saying.

From **Level 4** (Recognise that accounts of the past often disagree for valid reasons — as in Macaulay's poem about Naseby and Yeames's picture — 'Wrong but Romantic') to **Level 7** (Demonstrate an awareness of the relationship between historical accounts and the sources used to compile them — as in Elizabethan seamen's descriptions of Negroes and Spaniards,) *TELLTALE* speaks for itself. Using these materials an average class of Juniors will hit AT4 at Level 8 (Synthesise a wide range of complex and disparate information about an historical problem to produce a coherent and balanced explanation — for example, to explain why Charles I failed to escape from Carisbrooke Castle.)

It is a special feature of *TELLTALE* that primary sources are repeatedly matched with modern imaginative reconstructions, narrative paintings and Victorian patriotic poems. These inevitably lead pupils towards a recognition "that people influence interpretations of an historical issue in specific ways." and "vary according to time and place" **(Level 6)**. Reference to the stories' far-reaching content and to the investigative technique of **Appendices A** and **B** will convince experienced Primary school teachers that most of their pupils will be able to interpret the stories' evidence confidently to **Level 7:** (an awareness of the relationship between historical accounts and the sources used to compile them — as in Lady Brilliana's letters to her son.) **(Final Report pp. 129-30)**. The New Curriculum demands far less than this. *TELLTALE* speaks for itself.

Attainment Target 3: Acquiring and evaluating historical information is of the very essence of all *TELLTALE* books. Investigation is directed immediately and continually towards this target, beginning at **Level 2** (information from more than one type of source) as we follow a hostage's despatches from the North, a pirate's journal, a terrorist's forced confession, personal diaries, letters and logbooks, even an exercise in deciphering a 17th century letter in code.

Carefully graded questions lead pupils confidently through **Level 3 (a)** (Acquire information from a variety of sources which contain more information than is needed for the specific task — as in Pepys's incidental detail of Restoration costume) towards **Level 4 (a)** (Recognise which types of historical source might be useful for a particular line of enquiry — matching building *Prospects* of London with written descriptions of the Great Fire) and **(b)** (Recognise some problems inherent in using a range of sources, — as in the conflicting reports of Hawkins's disastrous Third Voyage) and **Level 5** (examine a variety of sources of evidence in terms of their contribution to an historical enquiry — assessing the evidence for and against Raleigh at his trial and rejecting more recent accretions, like *The Boyhood of Raleigh* which are imaginative but irrelevant.)

Mature pupils of all ages will soon progress through **Level 6**: (Compare critically and cross-reference sources as evidence or historical issues — such as the continual failures of the Royalist army.) to **Level 7**: (Recognise that the value of sources is determined largely by the questions asked about the evidence — as in our acceptance or rejection of the Gunpowder plotters' forced confessions.) It was a nine-year-old boy who once remarked about the Factory Commissioners' Reports: "If this man goes on asking this sort of question, he will always get this sort of answer."

Attainment Target 4: Organizing and communicating the results of historical study. It is an essential feature of *TELLTALE*, that Primary school teachers are encouraged to organize their own classroom strategies to investigate and reconstruct the evidence of the stories. We suggest, throughout, that teachers encourage discussion, in groups and as a class response. The folder of pictures, maps and diagrams offers other suggestions for notes and records and the matching of one kind of evidence with another, such as archaeological relics and museum artefacts, visits to historic sites and houses. The activities suggested in **Appendix B** also recommend criteria for reconstruction, drama and role-play based upon "an uncompromising respect for evidence." **(Final Report 10.5: p.177).**

In fact, *TELLTALE*'s teaching structures, discussion and record are equally applicable to Key Stages 1 and 2, both more and less able pupils. In the Working Group's own words: "3.20: With sufficient care in selection, historical content from any period can be taught at a level appropriate to the understanding of pupils of any age." **(Final Report, (April 1990) p.10).**

The significance of stories from History is that they bring the real meaning of any period to the surface. All the historical themes and theories, of nationalism, Renaissance and Reformation are portrayed for us here, in terms of real people's actual behaviour. Henry VIII's dispute with Rome inevitably creates a schism which has deep significance, in terms of dogma and politics. To one boy in Essex it means a beating from his father; to the Lancaster Herald, uneasily aware that he has become a hostage, it is a matter of life and death - or just another difficult job to be done. To Elizabeth I and Philip of Spain, war becomes an extension of diplomacy; to Hawkins' marooned seamen it means 12 years at the oars of a galley. To a captive King, Civil War culminates in one's head, not yet on the block, but stuck in a barred window. Stories are History, happening to ordinary people.

When we move into the period of Early Modern Britain, in the 16th and 17th century, we see our History become more English. This happens in a literal sense, with the spread of secular education and the invention of printing, for, in new books, the very words of History are now translated for us. The Dark Ages had produced very little written evidence, the Middle Ages created a monopoly of monastic scribes sharing a common European academic language - Latin. The stories in this book are in the words of Englishmen writing in English and, in such cases as Foxe and Hakluyt, writing popular bestsellers.

In this respect Early Modern Britain creates new opportunities for attaining the targets of acquisition and enquiry. There is a whole new series of personal papers such as Lady Brilliana Harley's letters to her son, Raleigh's rules of manners for *his* son and Pepys's secret diaries. Seamen kept their logbooks and wrote their reminiscences in English; Guy Fawkes's confession is written down in his own words, not as a Latin deposition, Henry Firebrace's tale of Charles I's abortive attempt to escape from Carisbrooke Castle tells a story which children can understand, first-hand. Libraries are full of the vivid words of Tudor men and women and many of them have special significance to schools in Plymouth, Naseby, Hanley Castle or Herefordshire. A careful local search will not go unrewarded.

The English language of letters, despatches, diaries and broad-sheets of the 16th and 17th centuries is often oddly unfamiliar, with the sound of forgotten dialect. Some of our extracts have demanded more simplification for children than earlier, more straightforward translation of a Latin chronicle. We hear, in an account of the Pilgrimage of Grace how my Lord Darcy turned to the commons "assone* as they came to Pomfrett* and toke there part." Off the coast of Florida, preparing to attack a Spanish fort, Drake's lieutenant describes how "we forthwith prepared to have ordinance for the battery planted, which strake through their Ensign." Yet when Raleigh, writing aphorisms for his young son, tells him of the evils of strong drink, which "ruins your health, poisons the breath, overheats the stomach, spoils the face, rots your teeth and makes you old before your time", he is simply speaking English.

Even plain-speaking Pepys can perplex us when he quotes Sir George Carteret's complaint that "he was not for the Fanfaroons*, to make a show with a great title", adding that "the King shall not be able to whip a cat but I must be at the tayle of it". But when he merely describes his meeting with the Duke of York's men, just returned from sea, "all fat and lusty, and ruddy by the sun", he paints a clear word-picture, as when he notices the poor singed pigeons falling from the window-ledges of a burning London street. The important difference in all these new sources is that these story-tellers are telling their own tales, in their own words, about their own actions and experiences. The medieval chronicler was often reporting the hearsay evidence of illiterate barons and knights.

As to our target of *evaluating* historical information, these are clearly marked out in the sections which insist that every story-teller must be carefully interrogated, as we **Check the Evidence**. Each story raises its own special questions of viewpoint, possible exaggeration or bias and each is carefully tested. General criteria for verifying the authenticity of any other stories as evidence are more closely examined in **Appendix A**.

Children will find that, in some ways, this period's evidence is more straightforward than the earlier chronicles. Bias and prejudices are more plainly stated, and there is no hypocritical effort to cover up hostile attitudes, which we would denounce (or conceal) today as vanity, snobbery, racism or inhumanity. These narrators usually say exactly what they mean, even if they wrap it in circumlocution.

As to the essential targets of *understanding these other points of view*, these are clearly marked out, for teacher and pupil alike, in the sections which ask of every tale: **"What is your verdict?"** This is perhaps a less straightforward task for modern children than the mere understanding of the narrator's language and plot. We find ourselves dealing with a past which does indeed often seem to be a foreign land. Attitudes towards fellow men, particularly, as in the calm, amoral view of a totally unscrupulous trade in defenceless Negroes, will often seem quite incomprehensible, and certainly unacceptable by today's more wishful thinking. The criteria for arriving at some sort of judgement, not only of the authenticity of the evidence, but also about the behaviour of the people in the stories, are more closely examined in **Appendix B**.

As in the other books in this series, we also turn to the *interpretations* of an age other than our own - that of the Victorian painters and poets. Narrative paintings like Yeames's *"And when did you last see your father?"* remind us of a viewpoint which saw the Royalist cause as Wrong but Romantic; Macaulay's poem on Naseby may, unwittingly, complete the picture of Roundheads who were Right but Repulsive. By introducing this different perspective we also share a colourful, imaginative understanding of the past which children can compare with our modern attitudes.

We perceive the three main themes of this period as Change, Discovery and Courage in face of the unknown. The last feature will demand more understanding on the part of modern children. It is a sad reflection that so much vivid action in these stories, as in the earlier periods, is concerned with violence. Indeed, though we must repeatedly acknowledge the rough courage of seamen or rebels, it is usually courage in the face of unnecessary danger. The courtier and the martyr demonstrate grace under pressure, as one kneels to the axe and the other feels the fire; a chatelaine calmly defies a stronger besieging force who, she is sure, will cut her throat and her children's too; plotters stand firm together in the courtyard of Holbeache as the sheriff's men gun them down. It is all a tragic commentary on man's inhumanity to man.

The Elizabethan buccaneers, it is true, show courage in facing unknown seas and mysterious lands. Trusting in Providence, they vow to "Serve God daily, Love one another, preserve our victuals, beware of fire and keep good companie." - Fear God and keep your powder dry! - Praise the Lord and pass the ammunition! It never changed. Yet, regularly and often, that simple courage turns to pillage and revenge. It takes a strange sort of courage to burn a simple, undefended village, just because it is there. We may need to develop a more careful vocabulary of what we really mean by bravery, gallantry, self-sacrifice and courage.

In later, more modern stories, we shall witness the courage of scientists like the Curies, whose unknown, as deadly as any other form of danger, is that of the scientist making a different sort of discovery. Later still, Scott in Antarctica or Armstrong and Aldrin on the moon, can be courageous without needing to use brute force on other people. Even so, it is a sad fact that History seems to make heroes only in adversity and, worse still, in violence. Sometimes, in this period especially, men create their own adversity, in which to behave heroically.

In this book, only Pepys has the opportunity to show a different sort of courage, that of the busy, conscientious man faced first with an epidemic that he feels sure has reduced his life expectancy to within the next two days. Busily, he sees to the safety of his wife and servants and the safety too, of his gold, his stocks of wine and parmesan cheese. Then, in his next adventure, walking the burning London streets with blistered feet, he worries as much about his office and his business papers as about the safe removal of his furniture by boat. For most of this time, however, we must accept a range of tales which deal entirely with troubled times, treason, and sudden death. The stories in this collection deal with three main political aspects of Tudor and Stuart life - religious strife, seafaring and civil war. Often these are inextricably woven together; causes of war with Spain emerge from English seafaring and English religion; religious differences cause the breach between Parliament and King. We see the development of our nation, the Tudor sense of God's Island, developing into the Stuart concept of the Commonwealth. The later conflicts of the Stuarts are deep-rooted in the earlier religious conflicts. They are forecast in some of the demands of the Northern Pilgrims, whose lost cause begins our book.

(Throughout the text of *TELLTALE,* * refers to a word in the Glossary.)

THE FLOWER OF THE NORTH

As Henry VIII's reign drew to a close, people began to feel the power of new Tudor monarchy. Government was in the hands of new men — upstarts, to the older generation. The King's chief minister, Thomas Cromwell, was most hated, but there were other causes of unrest. In villages throughout the land, the newly rich were making fortunes from the spoils of ransacked monasteries. They enclosed village commons for sheep-runs and turned their tenants out. New taxes and inflation impoverished some families whilst others grew rich on change.

The King himself had introduced unsettling changes, in his daughters' disputed succession, in local government, in methods of taxation and above all, in religion. Royal Commissions for every sort of unsettling purpose visited the shires and there was a growing suspicion of more damaging changes on the way. As the monasteries disappeared, with their many social services, people wondered if their own parish church might not be next for privatisation. In 1536 rebellion broke out in the Catholic North, combining many classes of folk with different grievances and different loyalties. They called themselves Pilgrims and their uprising is known as the Pilgrimage of Grace. It was the most serious crisis of Henry VIII's reign.

Ancient kings used to kill the messenger who brought bad news. Thomas Miller, the royal Lancaster Herald, sent to read the angry King's proclamation to the rebels, must have felt himself in danger from all sides.

As I approached the town of Pomfrett*, I overtook several companies of rebels who were common farming folk. They saluted me politely and gave great honour to the King's coat of arms which I wore. I asked them why they were in harness* and assembled in this way. They answered that it was for the common wealth*. They said that if they did not do so, the common people and the church would be destroyed. I asked them, how? They answered that no-one would be able to bury or christen anyone, nor wed, nor have their cattle unmarked, unless the King had a certain sum of money for every such thing. I told them how good and gracious the Lord King had been to them, how long he had kept them in prosperity and peace. I said that neither His Grace, nor any of his Council, ever thought of such ideas that they were complaining of.

With such persuasion as I said to them, riding into the town, I managed to get 300 or 400 of the common people to go, gladly, home to their houses and to ask the King's mercy. But they said they were weary of the life they were in. I went first to the Market Cross, where I should have made the proclamation*. Robert Aske, Captain of the host, being in the Castle, heard tell that I was come into town and sent for me to come to him, and so I did. As I entered the outer ward*, there I found many men in armour, very cruel fellows, and a porter, with a white staff in his hand. At both the other two gates, was another porter with a white staff and harnessed men. I was brought into the Hall, which I found full of people. I was told to wait there until such time as the traitorous Captain's pleasure was known.

I stood up at the high table in the Hall, and there showed the people the cause of my coming and the nature of the proclamation. While I was doing this, Aske sent for me to go to his Chamber. There, he kept his bearing and expression as though he had been a great prince, with great harshness, like a tyrant*. He was accompanied by the Archbishop of York, my Lord Darcy, Sir Robert Constable, Sir Christopher Danby and several others. As my duty was, I saluted the Archbishop and my Lord Darcy, showing them the cause I came for.

Then the said Robert Aske, with a cruel and proud expression, took the hearing of my tale. I told this with as much honour to our Sovereign Lord the King as common sense allowed. The said

Captain Aske paid no respect to it, suspiciously demanding to see my proclamation. I took it out of my purse and delivered it to him and he read it aloud, with no respect for any person. He said that he did not need to call any council to answer this, as he could, of his own knowledge give me the answer. Standing at the highest part of the chamber, and taking high estate upon himself, he said: "Herald, as a messenger, you are welcome to me and all my company. As for this proclamation, sent from the Lords, from whence you came, it shall not be read at the Market Cross, nor in any place amongst my people, who are under my guidance. Nor does the fear of loss of lands, or life and goods, nor the fear of the power which is set against us, enter our hearts. We are of one accord* with the Articles* of our demands, clearly intending to see an improvement, or else to die in this cause."

I asked him what these Articles were. He said that the first was that he and his company would go to London, on a pilgrimage to the King's Highness, there to have all the vile blood of his council put away from him and all the noble blood set up again. Also, the Faith of Christ, and his laws, to be kept, and the full restoration of Christ's Church and undoing of all wrongs done to it. Also, the common people must be used as they should be. He bade me trust to this, that it would be done or he would die for it. I asked him to give me this in writing, for my memory would not serve to carry it all away. He said, "With a good will!" and called for his Oath, which he read to all his people. He delivered it, in writing, to me and made me read it myself. He said that he would set his hand* to that, and die in the quarrel and his people with him. Then I prayed him to put his hand to the said Bill*, and so he did. With a proud voice, he said: "This is mine Act, whosoever sayeth to the contrary."

He said that he meant no harm to the King's person, but to see reform done. I fell on my knee before him, explaining that I was only a messenger, charged* by the King's Council to read the proclamation which I had brought. He answered that, on my life,

I should not read it. For he would have nothing put into his people's heads that should go contrary to his intentions. He said that I should have, at all times, his safe conduct to come and go with messages, whether wearing the King's coat-of-arms or not. He said that if my Lord of Shrewsbury, or any others of the Lords of the King's army came to speak with him, they too would have his safe conduct, to come safely and to go safely.

He also said: "Herald, recommend me to the Lords, from whence you come. Say to them that it would be fitting that they should support me, as I am doing this for all their good. He commanded Lord Darcy to give me 2 crowns* as a reward, whether I wanted it or not. He took me by the arm and brought me forth, out of the Castle, and there made an announcement that I must go safely and come safely, wearing the King's Coat, on pain of death. So he took his leave of me and went back into the castle, in high honour from the people, as a traitor may.

THE EVIDENCE

The Narrator: We can find out no more about Thomas Miller himself, but his office is still an important ceremonial rank in heraldry. The rank of six Ordinary Royal Heralds was founded by the first Tudor King, Henry VII, but the Lancastrian Heralds enjoyed a more ancient origin. Their office was first created at Calais in 1347 as a retainer of the noble house of Lancaster, and especially of John of Gaunt the most famous Duke, and his son, the Lancastrian King Henry IV. Under the Lancastrians, their Herald was promoted to the more senior rank of King at Arms, and was known as 'King of the Northern Province' until 1464, when he was reduced in rank. The Lancaster Herald's badge is still a red Lancastrian rose, royally crowned.

The Documents: There are many documents about the Pilgrimage of Grace in printed Calendars of State Papers, available in reference libraries. These have been printed as learned articles in historical journals which consider the Pilgrims' motives and weigh the importance of the various social, economic and religious causes of rebellion. The original documents include foreign ambassadors' observations, the reports of spies and secret agents, personal letters describing events in different regions, the rebels' own manifestoes and official despatches from Cromwell and the King's officers on the spot.

CHECK THE EVIDENCE

The Herald is trying to do several things at once. At the time of his visit to Pontefract he is obviously afraid for his safety, but also trying to do his duty. Aske and his men will not allow him to read the King's proclamation, but if he fails to give the King's message he will be in trouble later. His report to an angry King must give a truthful picture, but also make it clear that he maintained the royal dignity, giving no encouragement to the rebels. He might also be worried that, if he writes everything openly, his despatches might be opened by the rebels. He must be careful what he writes.

Study Miller's account and mark any phrases which seem to show the writer's feelings and fears. Can you see any threats against him? Does the story seem likely to be truthful and complete?

INFORMATION

Tudor rebellions: Henry VIII's religious Supremacy caused confusion as well as conflict. Englishmen resisted interference by Rome in English politics and finance. Yet, as we see in our next story, many folk clung to familiar Catholic beliefs. This was particularly true of Wales, whose people preferred old Latin service books to new English translations. Neither Henry nor people realised that the King's political disputes must lead to toleration of the Protestant religion.

Many folk sympathised with the misfortunes of Queen Catherine and her daughter Mary. Ann Boleyn's family was unpopular, and the King's divorce aroused opposition. Widespread anti-clericalism, aimed at the worldliness and occasional immorality of priests and monks, was confused by dependence upon the social services which the monasteries provided, and jealousy of the gentry who grew rich from dissolution.

Royal policy was ambiguous. Catholics like More went to the block for denying royal Supremacy, whilst Protestant commoners were burned for denying the Mass. Parliament was used by Henry VIII to pass Acts which severed connections with Rome, but Parliament would soon find other popular causes to support – one of the claims of the Pilgrims was to have a Parliament at Nottingham or York, "and that speedily".

The issues were aggravated by a long-standing north-south divide. The conservative, Catholic aristocracy of Lancashire, Yorkshire, Westmorland, and Cumberland opposed the Protestant beliefs of south-eastern counties. Central government was not as strong in the north, where great Earls ruled like kings before power passed to upstart councillors. It was the sickly Earl of Northumberland's disinheritance of his brothers in 1536, in favour of the crown and a pension, which first raised opposition. This was aggravated by dissolution of small monasteries in the same year; the monks were popular in the North, especially in Lincolnshire and Yorkshire, where the uprising began and in Lancashire, where it spread.

The Pilgrimage of Grace: began in Lincolnshire, where Commissioners taking taxes and suppressing monasteries were attacked. 40,000 rebels, including 800 monks and priests, rioted in Louth and Horncastle and occupied Lincoln. The Earl of Shrewsbury, Henry's commander in Nottingham, sent the Lancaster Herald to read a proclamation ordering the rebels to disperse, which they did. This was fortunate, as the royal armies of the Dukes of Suffolk and Norfolk were desperately short of men and arms. The King denounced the people of Lincolnshire, as "one of the most brute and beastly shires". He insisted that they had no right to criticise his Acts, passed in Parliament.

Robert Aske, a country gentleman and lawyer, taking the title of Captain, raised the East Riding and entered York with 10,000 men. Hull was taken and old Lord Darcy surrendered Pontefract Castle. Members of the King's local council placed themselves at the head of the rebellion, joined by the Archbishop of York. It was on October 21st that the Herald was received in Pontefract Castle by Aske. By 24th, 30,000 well-armed, mounted men, including nobility and gentry, wearing the badge of Christ's Five Wounds, mustered at Doncaster. News came that Lancashire had also risen in revolt.

Lacking armed support, his soldiers in sympathy with the rebels, Norfolk agreed to a truce. Independent representatives would take the rebels' grievances to the King in London, demanding a Parliament, with freedom of speech and no royal interference in elections. Princess Mary was to be made legitimate and the King was not to declare his successor. Care of souls must be reserved for Rome, and several ancient boroughs were to be reinstated. In modern terms, the rebels had agreed to accept arbitration. Norfolk told Henry that he had no intention of keeping any promises he made.

On the basis of the King's most gracious, free pardon, the armed host, described as the Flower of the North, dispersed, victims of an outrageous bluff. With the birth of a son and heir in 1537, Henry VIII was more powerful than ever. After an abortive rising under Captain Poverty in Westmorland and Cumberland, martial law was proclaimed in the North and summary executions were carried out without trials. In June, Darcy was executed in London, in July Aske, at York; 20 leaders of the rising met the same fate. In all, 216 rebels suffered the death penalty, including one Lady Bulmer, who was burned.

WHAT IS YOUR VERDICT?

Strong government can make all sorts of unpopular changes, provided that only one section of the community is attacked at a time, and that other classes of the community profit from the change. It is only when several different classes of people, not normally much in sympathy with each other, feel united in opposition to too many changes, that an uprising against the government becomes possible. Find out how many sections of the Tudor community in the North had grievances with which you too, are in sympathy.

If sensible opposition to government has no method of airing its grievances through normal channels, like law courts or Parliament, is it reasonable for them to take to the streets and impose their will on government by a show of force?

How far do you believe that the Pilgrims of 1536 were making only a show of force? Notice how readily they backed down at the offer of representatives to take their case to the King. Were they fairly treated by the King's commanders? What else could the Duke of Norfolk have done in his indefensible position?

Find out more about the character of King Henry VIII and his methods of dealing with opponents of his methods of government. How have modern dissidents been dealt with, in South Africa and Russia, for example?

From this uprising on, in Tudor times and afterwards, it was always the fashion for rebels to say that they were loyal supporters of a monarch who was being misled by false counsellors and that they knew that he would grant their requests, if they could only be allowed to bring them to his attention. How far was Henry VIII really at the mercy of counsellors like Wolsey and Thomas Cromwell? What happened to his Counsellors?

THE FLOWER OF THE NORTH

From this sort of beginning, how could the Tudor monarchy become so popular? From here onwards, England develops a sense of national unity such as it never had during the Middle Ages. What was the character of that nation going to be?

In 1534 Henry VIII made himself Head of the English Church. This created divisions amongst his subjects, Protestant against Catholic, which still cause strife and bloodshed in Northern Ireland today. Amongst other religious reforms, Henry, once Defender of the Catholic Faith, accepted a new English Bible and ordered that it be read in churches. Our next story tells that religious change was not always to the liking of the older generation and often divided families against each other. The author to whom the boy, William Maldon, told his tale in 1554, was John Foxe, who wrote a famous *Book of Martyrs* about the trials and troubles of early English Protestants. Most victims suffered violent pains for their faith. They were burned; William Maldon was lucky to escape with a beating.

When the King had allowed the Bible to be set forth, to be read in all the churches, immediately several poor men in the town of Chelmsford in Essex, where William Maldon's father lived and was born, bought the New Testament. On Sundays they sat reading it in the lower end of the church. Many would flock about them to hear their reading. William came every Sunday among the rest, being then only fifteen years old, to hear the glad, sweet tidings of the Gospel.

But his father, seeing this once, angrily fetched him away, and would make him say the Latin matins* with him. This grieved William very much. He still returned at other times to hear the Scriptures read and his father would still fetch him away. This made him think about learning to read English, so that he could read the New Testament for himself. When, by hard work, he had managed this, he and his father's apprentice* bought the New Testament by putting their pocket money together. They hid their Bible under the bed-straw and read it secretly at convenient times.

One night, his father being asleep, he and his mother happened to be talking about the crucifix. William spoke about the customs of people kneeling down in front of it and knocking their breast with it when praying or raising their hands to it when it passed by in procession. This, he told his mother, was plain idolatry and against God's commandment, when He said: "Thou shalt not make any graven image, nor bow down to it, nor worship it." His mother, furious with him for saying this, said: "Wilt thou not worship His Cross, which was above thee when thou was christened and must be laid upon thee when thou art dead?" In the heat of this argument, mother and son went to their beds.

The result of that evening's conversation she soon repeated to her husband which he, impatient to learn. Boiling in fury against his son for denying the worship due to the Cross, he rose up forthwith and went into his son's room. Like a mad zealot*, pulling William by the hair of his head with both his hands, he pulled him out of bed and whipped him unmercifully. The young man bore this beating, as he told me, with a kind of joy, considering it was for Christ's own sake, and shed not a tear. His father, seeing that, was even more enraged, and ran downstairs to fetch a rope. He put it around his son's neck, saying that he would hang him. At last, after much pleading by the boy's mother and his brother, he left his son almost dead.

THE EVIDENCE

The Narrators: We know no more of William Maldon than Foxe's story. He makes a second appearance in Foxe's Book, informing on a recusant* neighbour. Essex CRO* has no record of that name and date, though a William Maldon appears at Quarter Sessions in 1597-8 in connection with two housebreaking charges. Could this be the same man?

John Foxe (1516-87), famous English Protestant martyrologist, was born at Boston (Lincs) and entered Brasenose College at the age of 16. During Mary Tudor's Catholic reign, Foxe lived abroad, where he met John Knox and other Reformers. The first draft of his *Acts and Monuments* was published in Latin at Strasbourg in 1554 and was translated into English in 1563. When Elizabeth became Queen, Foxe returned to England and was appointed prebend* of Salisbury and vicar of Skipton. He lived in Grub Street, London, debarred from promotion in the Church of England by his refusal to wear a surplice. His book, in vivid prose, illustrated with horrific woodcuts of people burning, became famous as Foxe's *Book of Martyrs,* one of the strongest influences on ordinary English peoples' Protestant spirit and dread of the return of Roman Catholic religion.

Foxe's massive work begins with the introduction of Christianity to Britain in 63 AD, with tables of Saxon kings and bishops. He recounts the quarrels of medieval kings with the Papacy and explains the teaching of Wyclif and Hus. Mainly, he describes religious events of the reigns of Henry VIII, Edward VI, Mary Tudor and Elizabeth, arranged chronologically, as an almost annual chronicle. Foxe tells many famous stories, such as *The words and behaviour of Lady Jane Grey on the scaffold* - (as painted by Delaroche in 1834). He includes the letters of condemned men to their families before going to the stake. The saga ends in 1572, with the St. Bartholomew's Day Massacre.

Foxe's book is violently biased, described by Catholics as Foxe's *Book of Errors.* There were nine editions from 1563 to 1684, when the last ancient edition was published. Publication resumed from 1841 to 1877, the most famous edition being that of Rev. Josiah Pratt's 8 volumes in 1870. William Maldon's story is found in Vol.8. In 1658, Foxe's vast collection of original documents passed to his great-grand-daughter's husband, Sir Richard Willis, who lent them to John Strype. The manuscripts are now stored in the British Library.

John Strype (1643-1737): was the sickly son of a silk-maker from

Brabant, John van Strijp, who came to London and set up business in Strypes Yard, off Petticoat Lane. (Now Strype Street, E1) and became a freeman of the City and Master of his gild. His son John attended St. Paul's School and Jesus College Cambridge, which he left because it was too superstitious (i.e: too High Church for his liking.) Taking Holy Orders, he became minister of Leyton in Essex and wrote several Lives of the Protestant bishops, Aylmer, Parker and Whitgift. In 1725 he published *The Annals of the Reformation in England*. For this he used a great deal of Foxe's original documentary material, including the anecdote about William Maldon. Stripe has been derided by critics for serious errors in Latin and paleography* : "His lack of literary style, unskilled relation of materials and unmethodical arrangement render his books tiresome to the last degree."

CHECK THE EVIDENCE

This small anecdote is important because it shows by what a long and tortuous path a tale from the distant past must come. Was William Maldon's family trouble really as important as all that? Why do you think that the anecdote has survived so long?

Why did William Maldon's father object to his son reading an English version of the Bible which Henry VIII had allowed? Apart from the Scriptures, what did Maldon most object to?

Why are ordinary people like William Maldon and ourselves so difficult to trace in historical records? Make a list of all the available documents of your own identity which might still be found in 400 years time. What sort of person will they reveal?

Is this story likely to be true, or only Protestant propaganda? Does it make any difference to the authenticity of the evidence if we can find no other trace of William Maldon?

INFORMATION

The English Bible: Reformation began amongst scholars in Germany and Holland and later, amongst the English Lollards. In doctrine however, English churches were Catholic and services, prayers and lessons from the Bible were spoken in Latin. Ordinary folk, most of them illiterate, gained knowledge of Scripture from the spoken word, in folk-songs, mystery* plays and legends or from a parish priest who was sometimes little better educated than themselves. Coloured wall-pictures and stained glass windows of parish churches were also a vivid source of information to medieval folk. Portions of the Bible had occasionally been translated into English since Alfred the Great sponsored Anglo-Saxon work on the texts of the Gospels and the Psalms. Other parts were translated during the Middle Ages, the most important being the work of **John Wyclif (1329-84)**, who challenged much traditional doctrine. Such translations were forbidden by Rome.

Until the invention of printing, c1450, books were written as individual manuscript copies. By the 16th century, small printed books were no longer a rarity and 12 English towns had printing presses; there were 20 in Germany and 100 in Italy. Amongst the first printed works was a Gothic-lettered Bible by **Johann Gutenberg (1400-68)**, a German from Mainz, who replaced solid blocks of print with movable type. Gutenberg's Bible was printed in Latin in 1458.

In 1462, a *Poor Man's Bible* was printed on the Continent and became very popular in Germany, France and Holland during the last years of the 15th century. This consisted of 40 or 50 woodcut pictures, illustrating stories from the Bible with short captions in Latin or the vernacular. This book fell into disuse with the spread of other printed texts and increasing literacy.

The first printed version of the Bible in English was the translation of **William Tyndale (1492-1536)**, a Gloucestershire man. Forced to leave England because of his work on Bible translation, he travelled in Holland and Germany, where he met Martin Luther. Tyndale's translation of the New Testament and five Old Testament books was printed in Cologne and brought into England from 1525 to 1530. There they were burned. On Henry VIII's orders, Tyndale was arrested in the Netherlands. He was strangled and burned at the stake near Brussels.

Miles Coverdale (1488-1569) was a Yorkshire man and an Austin friar*, a friend of Thomas Cromwell, Henry VIII's unscrupulous chief minister. Coverdale broke away from the friars to become a Lutheran and lived abroad, printing the entire Bible at Zurich in 1535. In 1540 Coverdale also printed Archbishop Cranmer's version, the first English Bible to be published with royal authority, ordering its use in every parish church. Bible reading by women, labourers, apprentices and servants was forbidden, but permitted to noblemen and gentlemen, as long as they read quietly, without arguing, debating or expounding upon the Scripture. In 1557 a revised edition was printed in England under a royal monopoly. It was first to use Roman type, not ancient Gothic print. This version became popular in England and was known as the *Breeches Bible,* referring to Adam and Eve's fig leaves as **breeches**

Other rare versions are the *Wicked Bible* of 1656, which leaves the word **not** out of the Seventh Commandment; the *Treacle Bible,* which substitutes **treacle** for **balm** in Jeremiah; the *Murderers' Bible* (1801), which has this misprint for **murmurers** in Jude ch.16 and the *Wife Hater Bible* (1810), which prints **wife** for **life** in Luke xiv,26.

At the **Hampton Court Conference of 1604** , James I accepted the idea of a new *Authorised Version* , which was completed in 1611. A *Revised Version* was issued by a Victorian committee of Convocation in 1870. Since then there have been dozens of new editions, including the *New English Bible* (New Testament) of

1961, the *Good News Bible* of 1966, an American Version and a *Children's Bible,* edited by Arthur Mee in 1924.

Puzzle: Was Shakespeare a member of the committee of writers who contributed to the authorship of the *English Bible*? You probably know that the Elizabethans loved codes and acrostics. So, take one of the numerous spellings of the playwright's name as Shakspeare. Call this 4-6 for Shak = 4 and Speare = 6. Now turn to the 46th Psalm in the older Authorised Version's text. Count 46 words in from the beginning and write down the 46th word. Now count 46 words back from the end. (Don't count the Hebrew punctuation-word Selah, if that is the last word). Now copy that - to find the hidden name of the author?

WHAT IS YOUR VERDICT?

We have heard a great deal lately about banned and blasphemous books, printed overseas and sold in England. Why do Government and various communities object so strongly to their publication? Why did Tudor governments try to prevent people learning about religion in their own language? Were they to some extent right in view of the religious wars which followed? Is it possible to stop any knowledge from spreading, once it is known by some people? What sort of English government might permit the English publication of *Spycatcher* or forbid the publication of *Satanic Verses*?

Find out more about different historic phases of censorship, for example the Nazis' burning of banned books in Germany during the 1930s. What are the rights and wrongs of any official prohibition of various forms of information? How often has national security been used as the excuse for censorship?

Who are the best judges of what we should read? Ourselves? - Government? - lawyers and judges? - religious leaders? - juries of ordinary people? - scholars and experts? - commercial publishers? -

an official censor? - school-teachers? - children? - children's parents? Debate this.

Notice how attitudes of Tudor government change for and against the English Bible, from time to time. Find out more about how attitudes varied from one region to another. Why did these variations happen?

Notice the importance of education to the 15-year old William Maldon. He taught himself to read, so that he might learn from the Bible. What were your incentives for reading? The Bible is still the most widely published English book. How important do you feel it is to your own life-style or politics? Do you feel as strongly as William Maldon and his father? If not, why not?

Notice how both sides, Catholic and Protestant, had their martyrs (as indeed they have today), who all died bravely for their beliefs. What does this teach you about the value of martyrdom? What do you feel about men like Tyndale and Coverdale, who escaped abroad?

Discover the nearest Catholic school in your town which has a martyr's name and find out more about him/her.

What are the present issues which divide and disrupt the Church of England? What is the position of women in the Church? How important will those issues seem in 400 years time? Who are the 20th century martyrs?

THE VOYAGES OF DISCOVERY

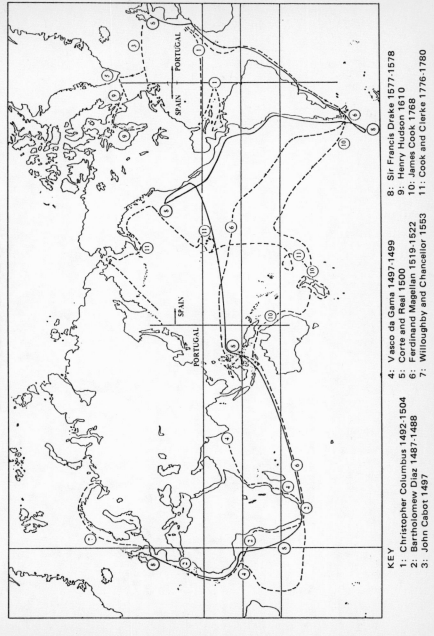

KEY

1: Christopher Columbus 1492-1504
2: Bartholomew Diaz 1487-1488
3: John Cabot 1497

4: Vasco da Gama 1497-1499
5: Corte and Real 1500
6: Ferdinand Magellan 1519-1522
7: Willoughby and Chancellor 1553

8: Sir Francis Drake 1577-1578
9: Henry Hudson 1610
10: James Cook 1768
11: Cook and Clerke 1776-1780

AN ELIZABETHAN PIRATE

The first Elizabethan Age was a time of discovery and exploration of a New World. England's island tradition gave an advantage to English ships and seamen, but Portuguese and Spaniards were first overseas. Their Catholic faith aggravated rivalry at sea. Elizabeth I's captains were staunch Protestants, but their motives for piracy and slave-trading were less admirable than their undoubted courage. Richard Hakluyt, working in Paris, grew tired of foreigners boasting of their travels. In the year after the Armada's defeat, he published a book of Principal Voyages and Discoveries of the English Nation. Here is part of his account of *"Master John Hawkins' Third Troublesome Voyage"*, in 1567-8.

Our ships set sail from Plymouth on the second day of October, 1567 and had reasonable weather until the seventh day. Then, forty leagues* North from Cape Finisterre, there arose a violent storm, which continued for four days. The fleet was dispersed, and all our great boats lost. The *Jesus,* our chief ship, was in such a state that we thought it unable to survive the voyage. So we set our course for home, deciding to give up our mission. But, on the 11th of the month the wind changed to fair weather, and we were encouraged to continue our adventure.

We made for the Canary Islands where, according to plan, all our scattered ships met again at one of the islands, called Gomera. There we took on water, and sailed on towards to coast of Guinea. We arrived at Cape Verde on the 18th. November and landed 150 men, hoping to capture some Negroes. At first we got only a few, and those with great hurt and damage to our men, chiefly from poisoned arrows. Though these seemed at first to make only small wounds, yet all those who shed blood died in a strange way, their mouths locked shut for ten days before they died.

From there we spent some time on the coast of Guinea, searching carefully along the rivers, from the Rio Grande to Sierra Leone until 12th. January, in which time we had only gotten together 150 Negroes. Because of our men's sickness and the time of the year we had to move on, but did not have enough Negroes to take to the West Indies. At first we decided to sail on to the Coast of the Mines, hoping to find gold there.

A Negro came to us, sent by his King. His people were at war with other neighbouring Kings and he begged for our help, promising us that any Negroes captured in this war would be ours. We agreed and sent 120 men ashore. On 15th. January we attacked a town of 8,000 people belonging to their enemies but it was so well defended and strongly fenced that we failed to take it. We lost six men, with 40 wounded.

Our men ashore sent to me for more help and, considering the possible profit of our success, I went ashore myself. With the help of the King of our side we attacked the town by land and sea, setting fire to the houses, which were all thatched with palm-leaves. We captured the town, put the people to flight and took 250 prisoners, men, women and children. The Negro King of our side also took 600 prisoners of whom we hoped to have first choice. But, that night the King removed his camp and prisoners, leaving us with only the few we had caught ourselves.

Now we had between 400-500 Negroes, which we thought to be a reasonable number to take to the West Indies. We took on water and fuel and left Guinea on 3rd. February continuing at sea with a more difficult passage than usual, until 27th March, when we had sight of the Island of Dominica in 14 degrees latitude.

We coasted from place to place, trading with the Spaniards as we could, but with some difficulty because their King had strictly ordered all his Governors there by no means to permit any trade with us. We still had reasonable trade and courteous entertainment, from the island of Margarita to Cartagena, except at Capo de la Vela (where all the pearls come from). There, the

Treasurer in charge would not agree to any trade or allow us to take on water, defending his town with barriers and 100 Musketeers. He thought that he would force us, by starvation to surrender our Negroes. So, with 200 men we broke down their barricades and stormed the town with the loss of only two men. After the first volley of shot, the Spaniards fled, but the people came back secretly by night and bought 200 Negroes from us. In all other places the Spaniards were glad to see us and traded willingly.

We departed on 24th July, hoping to have escaped the season of storms, but passing the west coast of Cuba, off the coast of Florida, we were struck by a hurricane on 12th. August. The storm lasted four days and so battered the *Jesus* that we had to cut down her topmasts. Her rudder was also sore shaken and she leaked so badly that we were on the point of abandoning her. We made for the coast of Florida, but found no haven for our ships because of the shallow coast. In great despair, attacked by another 3-day storm, we made for the chief port of Mexico, Saint John de Ullua, which stands in 19 degrees latitude. There we hoped for a quiet place to take on food and repair our fleet. The next morning we saw enter the harbour 13 great ships. Understanding these to be the Great Fleet, I sent immediately to their General, telling him of my being here and warning him that before I would allow them to come into port there must be conditions for our safety and for peace.

I am in two dangers, forced to accept one of them. Either I must keep their Fleet from entering the port, which, with God's help I was very well able to do, or else let them in and fear their usual treachery. But, if I kept them out, they might be wrecked in the storms, a Fleet which amounted in value, in our money, to £1,800,000. I could not answer for that danger, fearing the Queen's Majesty's anger at so weighty a matter. I decided to accept the possibility of their treachery and sent them my conditions. These, the Spanish Viceroy* on board their Fleet agreed, should be both favourably granted and faithfully performed, for the better friendship of our Queen and their King. There were many polite words of how, passing the coast of the Indies, he had heard of our honest behaviour towards the inhabitants. Thus at the end of 3 days all was arranged and the Spanish Fleet entered the port, saluting each other as the custom of the sea demands.

From the mainland* they reinforced themselves with 1,000 men and planned to attack us. We noticed signs of their treacherous plans - weapons being moved from ship to ship, cannon brought to the island, large companies of men moving from place to place and many other signs. I sent to the Viceroy, asking what was meant by all this action. He promised to give orders to take away all suspicious things.

We were not satisfied with his answer, suspecting a great number of men to be hidden in a great ship of 900 tons, moored next to our Minion. I sent again to the Viceroy, sending the Master of the *Jesus,* who spoke Spanish. Seeing that his plans were discovered, the Viceroy captured our Master, sounded a trumpet and from all sides they fell upon us. They killed all our men ashore without mercy, only a few escaped aboard the *Jesus.* The *Minion* sailed off, but they came aboard the *Jesus,* being beaten off with the loss of many of our men. We cast off our mooring ropes and got loose. The fight became so hot on all sides that within one hour the Admiral of the Spaniards was sunk, their Vice-Admiral burned and another of their great ships also sunk.

All the cannon on the island was now in Spanish hands. With it they shattered the masts and yards of the *Jesus,* so that there was no hope of sailing her again. They also sank all our small ships. We placed the *Jesus* between the Spaniards and the *Minion* to keep the *Minion* safe from the land-cannons and let her take off all food and stores from the *Jesus.* As we were doing this the Spaniards sent in two great fireships which were coming directly at us.

Having no way to avoid these, our men said we should depart with the *Minion*. Others said we should wait and see if the wind would take the fireships from us. Suddenly, the *Minion*'s men, who had their sails in readiness, sailed off without permission of their Captain and Master, so swiftly that I hardly had time to get aboard her. Most of the men left alive in the *Jesus* followed the *Minion* in a small boat, the rest were left to the mercy of the Spaniards (which I expect was very little). So, with the *Minion* only and the *Judith* (a small barke* of 50 tunnes) we escaped.

After this, sailing nearer to the cold northern country, our men, suffering from famine, died continually. Those that were left became so weak that we could hardly manage our ship, the wind always being wrong for us to make towards England. Arriving on the last day of December in a place near Vigo, called Ponte Vedra, our men fell into miserable diseases from over-eating fresh meat, so that many of them died. Knowing that the Spaniards saw our weakness and would attack us, we made all possible speed to sail to Vigo where we found help amongst some English ships, including 12 fresh men. We repaired our damage and filled our needs as best we might. Departing the 20th January 1568 we arrived in Mounts Bay in Cornwall the 25th of the same month, praised be to God therefore.

THE EVIDENCE

The Narrators: **Richard Hakluyt (c1552-1616)** was born in Herefordshire of Dutch ancestry. Educated at Westminster School and Christ Church, Oxford, he read theology but was more interested in the study of the world and universe. Taking Holy Orders, he lectured in geography and introduced the globe into English schools. At Oxford he studied accounts of voyages, in Greek, Latin, Spanish, Portuguese and French. His first book, *Divers Voyages touching the Discovery of America,* was published in 1582. It attracted the attention of the Queen's High Admiral, Lord Howard, whose brother, Lord Stafford, made Hakluyt his chaplain. As Ambassador, Stafford took Hakluyt to Paris, where he became concerned with English exploration, writing *A Discourse concerning Western Discoveries*. Returning to England in 1588, he began work on *Principal Navigations, Voyages and Discoveries of the English Nation,* collecting evidence from friends like Drake, Hawkins and Frobisher. In 1590 he was appointed rector of Wetheringsett in Suffolk and in 1604 archdeacon of Westminster, but continued to influence seafaring, especially encouraging colonisation in Virginia. He died in 1616 and is buried in Westminster Abbey. The Hakluyt Society was founded in 1846 to publish rare records of voyages, including the journal of Christopher Columbus. *Principal Navigations* was published in 1589 and re-issued in 1600. There have been several modern editions, by R.H. Evans in 1809-12 and W. Raleigh in 1903-5. Selections are printed in *An English Garner* (Ed: C.R. Beazley, 1903) and by E.J. Payne in *Voyages of the Elizabethan Seamen to America* (1893). These are available in reference Libraries.

Hakluyt's sources: Hakluyt faithfully transcribes the evidence of the sea-captains, navigators and seamen. The records of day-by-day navigation seem as if taken by reference to navigation log-books. An account of Hawkins's first voyage in 1564 concludes: "The Register and true accounts of all herein expressed hath been approved by me, John Sparke the younger, who went upon the same voyage, and wrote the same." Versions of Hawkins' third voyage were written by three survivors who had been marooned in Mexico. Job Hartop, gunner of the *Jesus*, was captured by the Spaniards and served for 12 years in the galleys. David Ingram, a sailor from Barking in Essex, went on his travels all over America but his tall stories were omitted from Hakluyt's later editions. Miles Philips, returned in 1583, having been "in their bloody hands" for 16 years. Hawkins own *Declaration of the Troublesome Voyage* was printed separately in 1569 and included in Hakluyt's 1589 edition. It was reprinted in full by Payne, from whose 1893 edition our story is abridged. Printed State Papers give the official version of the losses at Vera Cruz. We learn that

AN ELIZABETHAN PIRATE

Hawkins accused Drake of desertion in the *Judith,* a charge that haunted Drake for many years. We also learn that when Hawkins put 96 seamen ashore, not all of them were volunteers. Some were forced to swim ashore, more than a mile in rough seas. Each man was given a bolt of cloth, money and a farewell embrace from their General. Hawkins kept 100 African slaves aboard - they were more profitable than his sailors.

CHECK THE EVIDENCE

Do you dispute the Elizabethan seamen's courage? Has that judgment anything to do with their reliability as historians? What sort of men were they in terms of truthfulness and intelligence?

How far would Protestant resistance to Catholic Spain and Portugal affect their task as reporters? In view of the year of Hakluyt's publication, how suspicious must we be of his accounts as propaganda?

Can you detect any false statements in Hawkins's story? Look carefully, for instance, at what he says about his friendship with Spain and his intentions regarding Spanish treasure-ships.

INFORMATION

The Slave Trade: Black slaves had already been introduced into Europe from West Africa during the 15th century. The trade was begun by Arab merchants and Portuguese explorers of the West African coast, and was rapidly taken up by Dutch, British and French merchants. African states such as Dahomey, Ashanti and Benin, were also involved in the slave trade, Hawkins's story gives an example of tribal warfare which provided captives for the slavers. In the 1520s massive transportation to the New World began. From 1526 to 1870, 10,000,000 slaves were removed from Africa to Brazil, Spanish America, the British Caribbean and North America.

SIR JOHN HAWKINS

Spain and Portugal: By the late 15th century the Portuguese had claimed the Atlantic islands, the Gulf of Guinea and fortified factories* on the west coast of Africa. They bartered slaves and gold for cloth and hardware. The Papal demarcation of 1494, turned them towards the East Indies spice trade, to Malacca and Nagasaki, with limited slave and tobacco trade westward to Brazil. Spain controlled Spanish Main, Florida, Caribbean islands, and the Pacific coasts of Peru and Chile. An annual Great Fleet transported emigrants, returning to Spain with treasure. These were merchantmen, not warships; Hawkins's small, weakened squadron, could deny 13 great ships entry to Vera Cruz. It was no wonder that the Spaniards treated English seamen as pirates and heretics. To recent memories of Mary Tudor's Spanish marriage and Foxe's *Book of Martyrs* was added the aggravation of Spain's monopoly of Caribbean trade. The situation came to a head in the year of Hakluyt's publication.

Sir John Hawkins (1532-95): son of a sea-captain, was born in Plymouth. In 1562 he became the first Englishman to traffic in slaves, shipping 300 Africans from Sierra Leone to Hispaniola and trading them for hides, cochineal and sugar. In 1564, with the *Jesus of Lubeck, Minion* and two other ships, he took slaves to Venezuela, avoiding the Spanish embargo. These expeditions were proposed by groups of capitalists* who guaranteed funds, raised from friends at Court, including the Queen. Immense profits were paid out on a company shares basis. Later merchant adventurers formed themselves into Companies, trading with the Americas, Muscovy and East Indies. Hawkins's unscrupulous commercial career ended with the troublesome third voyage of 1567. Commanding the *Jesus* and five ships, including the *Judith,* commanded by his cousin Francis Drake, he plundered the Portuguese in Sierra Leone, captured 500 slaves and sailed for the Spanish Main. Returning home after the disaster, he secured the release of the sailors abandoned at Vera Cruz. He accepted a bribe of £40,000 to join the King of Spain's service, but remained loyal to Elizabeth. Hawkins always professed himself to be *an orderly* *man and a hater of folly* - a denial of piracy. His own account of his travels hardly confirms his opinion! Hawkins became MP for Plymouth in 1572 and Treasurer to the Navy in 1573, introducing several improvements. As Rear-admiral, he commanded the *Victory* against the Armada, kept watch on Dunkirk, held the Spaniards off the Isle of Wight and was knighted aboard the *Ark.* A ship-building partnership added to a fortune made from West Indian trade. In 1595, commanding an expedition with Drake to the Spanish Main, he died of fever at Porto Rico.

Elizabethan ships: were incredibly small. Drake's round-the-world voyage took no vessel of more than 100 tons burden. (Tunnage* is a difficult calculation; as a guide, Nelson's *Victory* had 2,150 tuns' capacity.) The *Squirrel,* which sailed to the colony of Newfoundland was only 10 tons - the size of a lifeboat. She sank on the return voyage. We can only wonder at the small space in which so many poor black folk were confined in stormy seas, for months on end. These were tubby vessels, carvel-planked with square rig and lateen mizzen sails, swift, manoeuvrable gun-platforms. Warships were larger, the *Triumph* of 1,000 tons, the *Revenge* of 500. The *Jesus* (700 tons) was a royal ship, lent to Hawkins with the *Minion.* The Queen begrudged her capital ships being endangered on the Atlantic. Her worst fears were justified by the fate of the *Jesus* in 1568. Hawkins' squadron comprised: HMS *Jesus:* 700 tons, 180 crew, 22 heavy cannon, 42 light guns. Captain J. Hawkins, Master Robert Barrett. HMS *Minion:* 350 tons, Captain John Hampton, Master John Garret. Private barks: *William and John:* 150 tons. Captain, Thomas Bolton, Master, James Raunce; *Swallow* 100 tons; *Judith:* 50 tons. Captain and Master Francis Drake (aged 22); *Angel:* 72 tons. The total complement of the squadron was 700 seamen.

Life at Sea: involved continual dependence upon dwindling stores of food and water and a limited knowledge of the oceans, based on inadequate maps and instruments. Hawkins admits to mistaking another island for Teneriffe and refers to *flitting* or disappearing islands. On course for Hispaniola, he loses Jamaica, misses the western end of Cuba and is driven onto the dangerous Florida shore. He was dependent upon French and Spanish members of the crew, Frenchmen and Spaniards, who had made the voyage before. They gave misleading information, recognizing all the wrong landmarks. Elizabethan seamen were fascinated by the strange sights they saw - crocodiles, flying fish, tortoises and unicorns - probably rhinoceroses. Armed shore-parties waded ashore from boats loaded with ships' cannon, enforcing commercial agreements and exacting high prices. Everything is taken at face value, with no moral view; cannibalism and slavery are taken for granted. Descriptions of the use of firearms on Africans, who had never seen bullet wounds and could not understand being shot, are distressing. Haggling the price of lean, sick Negroes, who would die aboard ship, seems to arouse no pity or remorse. This is the true spirit of the first Elizabethan age.

WHAT IS YOUR VERDICT?

It is usual for English History books to write of Sir John Hawkins that: "in spite of the cruel trade in slaves, he was a brave and worthy sea-captain". The facts of English piracy too, are glossed over in references to jaunty sea-dogs. Inhumane faults are matched against courage and seamanship. Is this balanced judgment a true or false idea? Can we say "*in spite of ...*", or do we have to make a simple right-or-wrong judgment?

Must we judge the issue of slavery in terms of 16th century attitudes which obviously saw no wrong in slave trading, or in terms of 20th century judgment on colonial exploitation of other people? In studying History, are we trying to understand other people, or ourselves?

More factually, do you find any other faults in Hawkins's behaviour? Notice how quickly he makes sure that he is aboard the survivors' ship at Vera Cruz, abandoning many of his crew to

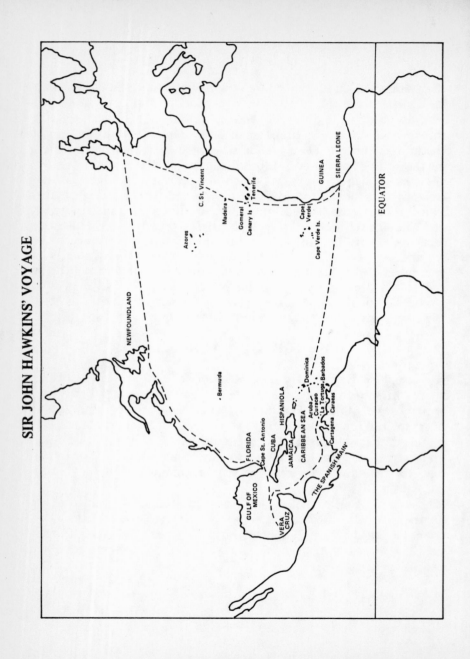

SIR JOHN HAWKINS' VOYAGE

NEWFOUNDLAND

C. St. Vincent

Madeira
Gomeral
Canary Is. Tenerife

Azores

Cape Verde Is.
Cape
Verde
Cape Verde Is.

GUINEA

SIERRA LEONE

EQUATOR

· Bermuda

FLORIDA
Cape St. Antonio
CUBA
GULF OF
MEXICO
VERA
CRUZ
JAMAICA
HISPANIOLA
CARIBBEAN SEA
Dominica
Aruba
Curacao
La Tortuga Barbados
Cartagena Caracas
"THE SPANISH MAIN"

the Spaniards ashore. What do you think of Hawkins' treatment of his own seamen?

How would we set about finding a Spanish description of Hakluyt's sea-dogs? How would we expect this to differ from our own story?

How shall we set about finding the African version of the slave trade? Use all available books and study units on the slave trade and Afro-Caribbean culture. Your local Library should have a list of these.

THE WORLD IS ROUND!

In 1961, Yuri Gagarin made the first manned orbit of the Earth in the Russian space-ship *Vostok I*. His single orbit lasted 89.34 minutes. But the world had been circumnavigated before, for the first time in 1522. A small fleet of sailing ships, under the command of the Portuguese navigator, Ferdinand Magellan, set sail from Spain in 1519. After a three year voyage one ship returned, without Magellan.

In 1961, shocked by the Russian achievement, the Americans entered the Space Race, determined to be first on the moon. In 1522, Englishmen too, were jealous of the discoveries made by Spain and Portugal in a New World. An English ship had sailed from Bristol as early as 1497, piloted by an Anglo-Venetian navigator, John Cabot, the first man of his generation to discover the mainland of America. Under Henry VII, England fell behind in the race; Cabot and the other explorers, Venetians, Genoese and Portuguese, turned to Spain for ships and money. During Elizabeth's reign, English seamen began to follow the sea-routes discovered - and defended - by their rivals. In 1577 the most famous of them all, Sir Francis Drake, set out secretly to become the first Englishman to sail around the world. His three-year voyage was recorded by his companions. Our version is abridged and simplified, but otherwise not altered.

On the 15th day of November, in the year of our Lord 1577, Master Francis Drake, with a fleet of 5 ships and the number of 164 men, both gentlemen and sailors, departed from Plymouth, giving out his pretended voyage for Alexandria. The wind falling contrary, he was forced the next morning to put into Falmouth haven in Cornwall, where such a terrible tempest took us, as few men have seen the like. It was indeed so fierce that all our ships were likely to be wrecked, but it please God to preserve us from that fate. Having brought the ships again to a good state, we set forth a second time from Plymouth, and set sail the 13th. day of December following.

The 25th day of the same month, we fell in with Cape Cantin, upon the Barbary Coast. Coasting along, on the 27th. day we found an island called Mogador, lying one mile distant from the mainland. Between this island and the main we found a good, safe harbour for our ships to ride in. The 17th. day of January, we arrived at Cape Blanco, where we found a ship riding at anchor and but two simple mariners* in her. We captured this ship and carried her further into the harbour, where we remained for 4 days. In that time the General mustered and trained his men on land in warlike manner, to make them fit for all occasions. We sailed by the island of St. Jago, far enough from the danger of the inhabitants, who shot three guns at us, but they all fell short and did us no harm. The island is fair and large and inhabited by the Portugals, but the mountains are said to be possessed by the Moors, who, having been slaves to the Portugals, escaped to the deserted parts of the island, where they live in great strength.

Off this island, we espied two ships under sail and gave chase to one of them. In the end we boarded her from the ship's boat without resistance. We found her to be a good prize, yielding us a good store of wine. The General gave her into the keeping of Master Doughty, and, keeping the pilot with us, sent the rest off in the pinnace with a butt of wine, some food and clothes. From the first day of our departure from the Islands of Cape Verde, we sailed 54 days without sight of land. The first land we sighted was the coast of Brazil, which we saw on the 5th April at 33 degrees. Being sighted by the inhabitants, they made great fires on the coast for sacrifices to the devils by which they do to cause storms and tempests to rise and carry away ships and men.

The seventh day, in a mighty storm of lightning, rain and thunder, we lost the *Christopher,* but on the eleventh day after, thanks to our General's great care in dispersing his ships, we found her again. The place where we met our General called the Cape of Joy, where every ship took in some water. Here we found a good temperature and sweet air, a fair and pleasant country with a very fruitful soil and many large and mighty Deer. We saw no people, but travelling further into the country we found footprints in the clay, showing them to be men of great size. From hence we went on our course to 36 degrees and entered the great River Plate, running into 54 fathoms of fresh water and many seals. Our General being on shore in that place, the people of the country came and showed themselves to him, leaping and dancing, and entered into barter with him. They would not take anything from our hands, the goods must be thrown on the ground. They are clean and handsome, with strong bodies, swift on foot and seem to be very active. There we watered and took in new provisions, especially seals of which we slew 200 or 300 in the space of an hour.

Here, our General in the Admiral, rode close aboard the *Swan* fly-boat* and took off all her provisions of food and whatever else was in her. Hauling her on land, he set fire to her, but kept the ironwork. Some of the men of the country came down while we were doing this. They were naked except for skins with fur on them around their waists and some on their heads. Their faces were painted in many colours and some had horns on their heads. Every man had a bow an in length and a couple of arrows. Our General being ashore, and they dancing after him in their usual manner, when he once turned his back on them, one jumped suddenly at him and took off his cap with its gold band. He ran off and shared it with his companion, one wearing the cap, the other the band. On the 20th. June, we harboured ourselves in a very good harbour, called by Magellan Port St. Julian. There we found a gibbet* standing on the shore, which we supposed to be the place where Magellan executed some of his disobedient and rebellious company.

In this port our General began to investigate the actions of Master

THE WORLD IS ROUND!

Thomas Doughty and found them tending to mutiny or some other disorder, whereby the success of the voyage might greatly have been hazarded. Whereupon, the company was called together and told of the particulars of the case, found out partly by Master Doughty's own confession. Which, when our General saw, although his personal affection to Mr. Doughty was great (as he then in presence of us all, sacredly protested) yet, the care he had for the state of the voyage, of the high hopes of Her Majesty and of the honour of his country, concerned him more than the private respect of one man. So, the case having been thoroughly heard in good order as near as might be to the course of our laws in England, it was concluded that Mr. Doughty should be punished according to the nature of the crime. He, seeing no remedy but patience for himself, desired before his death to receive Communion, which he did at the hands of Mr. Fletcher our Minister and the General joined him in that holy action. The place of execution being made ready, he embraced the General, taking leave of the company, with prayers for the Queen's Majesty and our realm. Then he quietly laid his head on the block, where he ended his life. This being done, our General made speeches to the whole company, persuading us to unity, obedience, love and care for our voyage.

The 17th day of August, we departed the port of St. Julian and the 20th day we fell in with the Strait of Magellan, going into the South Sea. On the 21st we entered the Strait, which we found to have many turnings and dead ends, as if there were no clear passage at all. We had the wind often against us, so that some of the fleet recovering a Cape or point of land, others were forced to turn back again and anchor where they could. The land on both sides is very huge and mountainous, the mountains covered with snow, the strait extremely cold, with frost and snow continually. The trees seem to stoop with the burden of the weather and yet are green continually and many good, sweet herbs grow plentifully under them. The 24th. August we arrived at an island in the strait where we found a great store of fowl which could not fly, about the size of geese. In less than one day we killed 3,000 and victualled* ourselves thoroughly with them. The 6th. day we entered the South sea at the Cape. The seventh day we were driven by a great storm 200 leagues* southward of the Strait. Coming back to the strait we ran, supposing the coast of Chile to lie, as generally maps have described it, namely north-west. Instead we found it to lie to the north-east and eastward. Whereby it appears that this part of Chile has never been truly discovered before, either set down on purpose to deceive, or from ignorant guesswork.

We set sail towards the coast of Chile and, drawing near it, met, near the shore, an Indian in a canoe. Thinking that we were Spaniards, he came to us and told us that at a place called St. Jago there was a great Spanish ship, laden from the kingdom of Peru. For which good news, the General gave him some trinkets, with which he was pleased, and went along with us to lead us to the place which is called the port of Valparaiso. When we arrived we found the ship riding at anchor, with 8 Spaniards and 3 Negroes aboard. Thinking that we were Spaniards and friends, they welcomed us with a drum and made ready a butt of Chile wine to drink with us. As soon as we went aboard, one of our company called Thomas Moone began to lay about him and struck one of the Spaniards, saying "Abaxo Perro!", which means, in English "Go down, you dog!". One of the Spaniards, seeing what sort of person had arrived, started to cross and bless himself. We stowed them all under hatches, except one Spaniard, who jumped overboard and swam ashore to the town of St. Jago, to warn them of our arrival. Those in the town, which was no more than 9 houses, fled away and abandoned the town. Our General manned his boat and the Spanish ship's boat and went to the town. We rifled* it and came to a small chapel, which we entered and found therein a silver chalice, two cruets and an altar-cloth, which our General gave to Mr. Fletcher, his Minister. We found a warehouse stored with Chilean wine and many boards of cedar-wood. We brought the wine away with us and burned the boards as firewood. Having come aboard, we left the harbour, having set the Spaniards ashore. When we were at sea, the General rifled the Spanish ship and found in her a good store of Chilean wine and 2,500 pesoes of very pure, fine gold from Bolivia, worth 37,000 ducats* of Spanish money or more.

At the next place, Coquimbo, our General sent 14 men ashore to fetch water. They were espied by the Spaniards who came with 300 horsemen and 200 foot soldiers, and slew one of our men with gunfire. The rest came safely aboard and the Spaniards departed. We went ashore again and buried our man. The Spaniards came down with a flag of truce but we set sail and would not trust them. Then we came to a port called Tarapaza, where we found by the sea-side a Spaniard lying asleep, with 13 bars of silver beside him, which weighed 4,000 Spanish ducats. We took the silver and left the man. We came to Lima on the 13th day of February and found, in the harbour, about 12 sail of ships fast moored at anchor, with all their sails carried on shore. For the masters and merchants were most secure, never having been attacked by any enemies here. Our General rifled these ships and found in one of them a chest full of *reals de plata** and a good store of silks and linen cloth. He took the chest into his own ship with a good store of the silks and linen. In which ship we had news of another called the *Cacafuego* which had gone towards Paita, laden with treasure. Staying no longer, we cut all the cables of the ships in the harbour and let them drive where they would, on sea or shore.

We sailed in pursuit of the *Cacafuego,* towards Panama. Our general promised that whoever should first sight her should have his chain of gold for the good news. John Drake, the General's younger brother, going up into the top, spotted her about 3 o'clock and about 6 o'clock we came to her and boarded her and shot at her with three pieces of artillery and struck down her mizzenmast*. When we entered her, we found in her great riches, jewels and precious stones, 13 chests full of *reals de plata,* 80 pounds of gold and 26 tons of silver. The place where we took this prize was called Cape San Francisco, about 150 leagues from Panama.

At Guatulco we ransacked the town and in one house we found a pot as big as a bushel* full of *reals de plata,* which we brought to our ship. Thomas Moone, one of our company, caught a Spanish gentleman as he was fleeing from the town and, searching him, found a chain of gold about him and other jewels, which he took and let him go. At this place, the General set ashore his Portuguese pilot whom he had captured off the Cape Verde Islands out of the Maria of Portugal. We sailed on to the island of Canno, where the General beached the ship and mended and graved* her, then filled her with wood and water. The General thought it better not to return by way of the Straits, for two reasons. First, lest the Spaniards should wait there in great numbers and strength, whose hands, he being now left with only one ship, could not possibly escape. The other reason was the dangerous weather at the mouth of the Strait, with continual storms and blustering. He resolved therefore, to go forward to the Islands of the Moluccas and from there, to sail on the course of the Portugals by the Cape of Buena Esperanza.

The 5th. June, being in 43 degrees towards the Arctic Pole we found the air so cold and our men being grievously pinched with the same, complained of the extremity of it. The further we went, the more the cold increased. We thought it best to seek land, which we did at 38 degrees, where it pleased God to send us into a good fair bay, where we anchored. The people, dressed in deerskins, visited us with feathers and bags of Tobacco as presents. Their houses are digged about with earth, with cliffs of wood from the brim of the circle, joined at the top like a church steeple. We found herds of deer by the 1,000, mostly large and fat of body. Their King and his Guard made signs to our General to sit down, and made long speeches, asking that he would take their country and kingdom into his hands and become their king. They made signs that they would resign their right and title to him and become his subjects. Joyfully singing a song, they set the crown upon his head and enriched his neck with their chains. Wherefore he took the sceptre, crown and dignity of the said country into his hands in the name and to the use of Her Majesty.

Our General called this country *New Albion,* There is no part of the earth here that, when dug up, does not show probable gold or silver ore. On our departure, our General set up a monument of our having been there and of Her Majesty's right and title to the land. He set up a board, nailed on a great post, on which was engraved Her Majesty's name, the day and year of our arrival here, with Her Majesty's picture and coat of arms on a sixpence piece under the board, with the name of our General. It seems that the Spaniards have never been in this part of the country.

We continued without sight of land from 23rd. July to the 13th day of October following, when we fell in with some islands from which came a great number of canoes with 6 or 4 or 14 men bringing coconuts and other fruits. We continued our course by the islands of Tagulada, Zelon and Zewarra, being friendly to the Portugals, and growing great store of Cinnamon. On 14th. November we fell in with the Islands of Moluccas, where the General sent the King a velvet cloak as a present and token of his coming in peace, saying that he wanted nothing but trade and exchange of merchandise. The island of Ternate is the chief island of the Moluccas and its King is king of 70 other islands. The people are Moors* in religion, observing certain new moons with fasting, during which they neither eat nor drink during the day, but only at night. Not long before our departure they told us that there were ships as great as ours, not far off, warning us to beware. Hearing this, our Captain would stay no longer. From Java Major, we sailed for the Cape of Good Hope, which was our first landfall. We found the report of the Portugals to be most false, that it is the most dangerous Cape in the world, never without intolerable storms. This Cape is the most stately thing, and the fairest Cape

we saw in the whole circumference of the world. We passed it by
on 18th. June. We did not touch it, nor any other land, until we
came to Sierra Leone upon the coast of Guinea. We arrived in
England on 3rd. November, 1580, being the third year since our
departure.

THE EVIDENCE

The Narrators: Drake's voyage is well documented by those who
sailed with him. His chaplain, Francis Fletcher, wrote one
account, John Cooke of the *Marigold* wrote another which was
anti-Drake, and John Winter, captain of the *Elizabeth* and Drake's
Vice-admiral, also kept records. Several other contemporary
accounts were widely published, including *The World
Encompass'd,* by Drake's nephew Francis, who used Fletcher's
notes as his source in 1628. Thomas Maynard, captain of troops
and member of Drake's war-council, published *Sir Francis Drake,
his Voyage* in 1595 and Thomas Greepe's *True and Perfect News
of the Exploytes performed by Syr Francis Drake* (1587) includes
a ballad of the time. Another of Drake's soldiers, Robert Leng,
also wrote of Drake's "memorable service done against the
Spaniards in 1587". The Spaniards published their own version of
the expedition, which was answered in England by *A Libel of
Spanish lies* in 1596. Most remarkable of Drake's chroniclers was
the Portuguese pilot, Nuna da Silva, taken prisoner off the African
coast. An expert navigator, he knew the sea-route to Brazil and
carried his own charts and instruments. Invited to eat at Drake's
table, he became known to the Spaniards as the Captain's
favourite. Da Silva's logbook is a primary source of information
about life aboard the *Golden Hind.* He hoped that Drake would
send him home in the *Maria,* but he was set ashore at Guatulco,
then captured and interrogated by the Inquisition. His depositions
are another source of information about the voyage. Inevitably,
Hakluyt publicised Drake's exploits in his best-seller; this was a
16th century media event! Many of the original sources mentioned have been published in modern works, available in

reference libraries. The documents of Drake's life and voyages were published by John Barrow in 1843 and there are numerous more recent popular biographies of Sir Francis Drake.

CHECK THE EVIDENCE

We all know (or think we know) that the Earth is round, so it is far too easy for us to ridicule medieval scholars for their earlier beliefs. If we think for a moment, we will realise that they were using the only evidence available to them - the evidence of their own eyes - just as you do when you see TV pictures of a spherical Earth taken from space.

If you try to forget all you have read, or been told, and only look, you may see that the earth is flat and stationary where you live! It looks as if the sun moves across the sky and that we are at the centre, within the other planets. So much for that sort of evidence!

Magellan, Drake and Gagarin proved the shape of the Earth by experiment. What sort of extra technology do modern astronomers use, to prove their theories about the Earth's movement and the state of the Universe? Do they all agree?

By the time that Columbus and Cabot set sail, there were very few experienced seamen who feared that they might fall off the edge of the World if they sailed too far. Be careful not to assume that all earlier people were more stupid than ourselves.

Use a modern atlas to find the names of bays, straits and islands named after their early European explorers. Make your own map of these places.

THE WORLD IS ROUND!

INFORMATION

Early Trade: Most medieval European trade, like Marco Polo's expedition, moved eastward, overland to China, India and Persia. The western focal points of this trade were Constantinople, Venice and the Mediterranean. Trade routes were shared in the East with seafaring Chinese, Indian and Arab merchants; in the north, with the Hanseatic League of the Baltic Sea. Medieval commodities included pepper, cloves, nutmegs, cinnamon, furs and hides, mace, cotton cloth, silks, carpets, perfumes, porcelain and jewels. During the 15th. century, the Turks attacked these eastern land routes and captured Mediterranean ports, forcing Europeans to look for alternative sea routes. Other crises, like plague, piracy and Chinese conquests also affected trade. European merchants needed ships' holds to carry gold and other goods too cumbersome for camels.

Exploration: Europeans were not the only seamen of the 15th-16th centuries, though their voyages under sail were most far-reaching. There was already limited navigation of the Pacific coasts of Ecuador and Peru and in the Caribbean by canoes and rafts. Apart from Spanish galleons and *"Portugals"*, canoes were the only craft encountered by Magellan and Drake across the oceans of the world. In the East, Arab, Indian and Persian dhows* sailed the Indian Ocean; Chinese junks*, numerous in the China Seas, did not sail further east than the Phillippines. The Chinese had occasionally reached East Africa but were usually confined to the Malay archipelago, sailing no further west than Malacca. There they shared trade with the Javanese, who had once sailed as far west as Madagascar. There was no shipping in the southern Indian Ocean towards Australia, and the Pacific was crossed only by flimsy, adventurous Polynesian canoes. (The Polynesians are now the world's most widely distributed ethnic group.) The only ships in the North Pacific confined themselves to the coast of Japan.

THE WORLD IS ROUND!

It was European exploration, from 1480 to 1780 which linked these oceans, continents and islands. Spanish and Portuguese explorers and their Italian navigators demonstrated that all the oceans of the world are connected. English History books usually emphasise Britain's sea-going advantage from our off-shore, North Atlantic island. This was an advantage shared first by sailors from the coast of Portugal. The first voyages were sponsored by the Portuguese Prince Henry the Navigator, in the 15th. century. He sent merchants to the African coast, searching for gold and slaves to man his sugar plantations in Madeira. By 1488 Bartholomew Diaz had reached the Cape of Good Hope, and in 1497-99 Vasco da Gama rounded the Cape to reach India.

The Spaniards sailed westward, to the far coasts of South America, which Drake plundered, whilst the Portuguese sailed eastward to the Indies. Columbus, a Genoese employed by King Ferdinand of Spain, in 1492, confused the Portuguese by sailing westward and claiming to have discovered India. He had, in fact arrived at the Bahamas, explored Cuba and called it China. Amerigo Vespucci merely followed Columbus's route, to explore the coast of Guiana. Later map-makers named America after him, misled by Vespucci's tales of fictitious voyages. In 1519-22 Magellan sailed westward from Spain, via the Canary Islands, down the coast of Brazil, to the southernmost tip of South America. There he discovered the Magellan Straits which led him into the Pacific Ocean. Sailing on to the Phillippines, Magellan and 27 of his men were killed by the inhabitants. Only one of his ships, the Victoria, sailed on via Java and rounded the Cape of Good Hope westwardly for home.

Sir Francis Drake (1540-96): was born on a farm near Tavistock, in Devon. His father was employed by the Duke of Bedford, who stood as Francis's godfather. Drake's family was strongly Protestant, forced by a West country rebellion against the new Prayer Book's "Christmas game" to leave home and seek refuge in a hulk* on the Medway. Drake's father became preacher to the Navy at Chatham, and, at fourteen, Francis joined the crew of a

SIR FRANCIS DRAKE

small Channel coaster. He became so competent a seaman that the Master left him his ship when he died. As a staunch Protestant, Drake was fortunate to be at sea during Mary Tudor's reign. When Elizabeth became Queen, he returned to Devon, a stocky, red-faced sailor, and sailed with his kinsman, John Hawkins on expeditions to Guinea and the West Indies. After the disaster at San Juan de Ulua (Vera Cruz), Drake began a vendetta against the Inquisition and the King of Spain, to whom he became notorious as *El Draque* - The Dragon. In 1577, his most famous expedition gained him a knighthood and popular acclaim.

In 1585 Drake took 25 ships to harry the Spaniards at Hispaniola, Cartagena and Florida, bringing home Raleigh's unsuccessful Virginian colonists with their tobacco and potatoes. In 1587 he sailed into Cadiz harbour and destroyed 33 Spanish ships. When the Armada appeared, Drake, as Vice-admiral of the English fleet, was stationed off Ushant, until storms drove all the English ships towards Plymouth. He captured the *Roario* off Portland, adding to his fame and popularity, but was forced by shortage of ammunition to give up the chase of the surviving Spanish ships. Drake became MP for Plymouth, where he organized the town's water supply. In 1595 he joined Hawkins in another piratical expedition to the West Indies, where he died of fever. Newbolt's poem *Drake's Drum* preserves the legend that in time of trouble Drake will be recalled to defend England again. The drum lies at Drake's house, Buckland Abbey, with his ship's pennants.

The Golden Hind: originally named *Pelican,* was Admiral-ship of the flotilla. Off the entrance to the Magellan Straits she was re-named in favour of Drake's sponsor, Sir Christopher Hatton. With dramatic ceremony, the figure-head was changed, the stern was embellished with the 14 quarterings of Hatton's coat of arms and the green and yellow top-sides were re-painted in his livery of red and yellow. Her length was 75 feet at the waterline, the deck was 20 feet wide and the mainmast 59 feet high. Fully rigged, the *Golden Hind,* a ship of only 100-150 tons, had a sail area of 4,150 sq.ft. At the mainmast St. George's ensign was flown, the Tudor flag of horizontal green stripes quartered with St. George's cross at the mizzen. The crew of about 90 men included officers, seamen, boys, musicians and tradesmen such as smiths, carpenters and coopers. On occasion the number was reduced to as few as 59. The ship carried several small boats or pinnaces, prefabricated in sections for erection ashore.

There were five decks, a lower gun-deck, the main deck, a half-deck with forecastle*, the quarter-deck* and a poop-deck*; the height between decks was 5ft.6ins. The 18 guns mentioned by da Silva were 14 demi-culverin* cannon of 4 " bore for 10lb cannon-balls and 4 breech-loading swivel or murdering guns in the bows. The ship was steered by a tiller on the gun deck, or by a whipstaff* on the half-deck above. Some officers had tiny cabins, but Drake insisted that they must "haul and draw with the mariners, and the mariners with the gentlemen. I want to know of anyone who refuses to set his hand to a rope." Drake's private cabin was on the half-deck above the Great Cabin, at the after end of the main deck. The Great Cabin could accommodate a conference of a dozen officers. Meals at Drake's table were formal, with music of viols*, gold plate and silverware. Drake's coat of arms, granted by Elizabeth I, was a globe with the north star passing over it.

Nuno da Silva described the *Golden Hind:* "The flagship is in great measure stout and strong. She has a double hull, the one as perfectly fashioned as the other. She is fit for warfare, a ship of the French pattern. She sails well and answers her helm. She is not new and is neither coppered nor ballasted. She has seven gun-ports on each side; inside she carries 18 pieces of artillery, 13 of bronze and the rest of cast iron, as well as an abundance of all kinds of munitions of war. She also carries workmen and a forge for making nails, spikes and bolts. She is watertight when navigated with a moderate stern wind, but in a high sea she labours and leaks not a little."

THE WORLD IS ROUND!

A special dock was built at Deptford in 1581, to preserve the *Golden Hind.* There she lay for 100 years, and Pepys himself went aboard her in 1662. The ship decayed and was broken up, but the Master Shipwright of the dockyard had a chair and table carved from her timbers. The chair stands in the Bodleian Library, the table at the Middle Temple in London. A replica was built in 1973 and sailed to Panama. Visit the actual-size version, moored at Brixham.

Drake's Fleet: included, the *Elizabeth,* vice-admiral ship of 80 tons, (Captain John Winter) which gave up and returned to England, having lost contact with Drake in the Magellan Straits; *Marigold,* bark of 30 tons: (Captain John Thomas), which disappeared off the Straits; *Swan,* fly-boat* of 50 tons: (Captain John Chester), sunk by Drake at Seal Bay on the coast of Argentina, as an encumbrance, and *Christopher,* a pinnace* of 15 tons: (Captain Thomas Moone), exchanged early in the voyage for a Spanish prize off Cape Blanc. Re-named *Christopher* she was abandoned, with the *Swan* at Seal Bay. Another Portuguese prize, *Maria,* da Silva's ship, taken off Cape Verde, accompanied the fleet. Re-named the *Mary,* she was captained by Thomas Doughty, later executed for mutiny; his ship, leaky and troublesome was abandoned, with Doughty's beheaded body, on the Isle of Blood.

WHAT IS YOUR VERDICT?

Modern textbooks often describe how European explorers *discovered* faraway lands, as though they had existed only to await the arrival of white men. Is this a racist attitude?

Sixteenth century explorers of all races were motivated by greed, out for profit at any cost. How did this damage the overseas environment and peoples? What benefits, if any, were offered in compensation? Drake's seamen, like Thomas Moone, often seem to behave like modern football hooligans abroad. Is this a national characteristic?

So-called *natives* and *savages* sometimes seem more peaceable people, with noble kings and grave councils, who fail to understand white men's violence. On the other hand, descriptions of painted, naked idol-worshippers, practising sacrifices and cannibalism, give different pictures of what others think of as noble savages. Can you explain these differences?

Do you think that Drake's assumption - without knowing the language of the people of California - that they wished to hand over New Albion to him and Queen Elizabeth was optimistic, if not unscrupulous? Why did nothing come of this take-over?

Did Drake treat Nuno da Silva fairly? Do you feel that Thomas Doughty had a fair trial? What impression do you gain of Drake - in modern terms? Are these fair terms on which to judge him? Was the Spanish Inquisition fair in its treatment of English heretic* prisoners?

THE SPANISH ARMADA

After the Catholic reign of Mary Tudor, England became a Protestant country once more. We saw in our last story how Elizabeth's buccaneers* pirated the gold-laden convoys on the Spanish Main and raided the New World trade of Spain and Portugal. In 1588, the Spanish King, Philip II, Mary Tudor's widowed husband, sent a great fleet with soldiers and the Pope's blessing, to invade England and convert it to the Catholic faith. His Armada was driven off by Drake, Hawkins and the English sea-dogs.

The rout of the Spanish Armada is described in detail, not only in Elizabethan State Papers, but also in letters from the Spanish Admiral to his King. He explains how the invasion of England failed and his fleet was scattered. The full account of the sea-chase and many useful papers, including Elizabeth I's own letters to her seamen, maps, ration scales and wages, are found in *The Great Enterprise* (Editor: Stephen Usherwood, Folio Society 1978). Here, with the Editor's permission, is a brief extract, adapted from the Spanish Admiral's long letter:-

The Duke of Medina Sidonia to Philip II on 11th. August 1588: On 22nd July, the Duke and the whole Armada sailed from Corunna with a SW wind which continued for the next few days, the voyage being prosperous. On the 30th, at dawn, the Armada was very near the shore. We were seen by the people on land who made signal fires, and in the afternoon the Duke sent Ensign* Julian Gil in a rowing-boat to obtain intelligence. In the afternoon a number of ships were sighted, but as the weather was thick and rainy, they could not be counted. Ensign Gil returned at night with four Englishmen in a boat, hailing, as they said, from Falmouth. They reported that they had seen the English fleet leave Plymouth that afternoon under the Lord Admiral of England and Drake.

On Sunday 31st, day broke with the wind changed to WNW in

THE SPANISH ARMADA

Plymouth Roads and 80 ships were sighted to the windward of us. Towards the coast to leeward 11 other ships were seen, including three large galleons* which were cannonading* some of our vessels. Our Armada placed itself in fighting order, the flagship* hoisting the royal standard at the foremast. The enemy's fleet passed by, cannonading our vanguard* which was under Don Alonso den Levy, then fell on the rearguard commanded by Admiral Juan Martinez de Recalde. The enemy attacked him so fiercely with cannon that they crippled his rigging, breaking his stay* and striking his foremast twice with cannon balls. The royal flagship then struck* her foresail, slackened her sheets* and lay until Recalde joined the main squadron. The enemy sheered off* and the Duke collected his fleet. This was all they could do, as the enemy had gained the wind, the English ships being swift and well-handled, so that they could do as they liked with them. Our Armada continued to manoeuvre until 4 o'clock in the afternoon, trying to gain the wind of the enemy. At this hour Oquenda's vice-flagship caught fire in its powder magazine, two of his decks and the poop-castle* being blown up. In this ship was the Paymaster General of the Armada, with a part of His Majesty's treasure. During the night the wind and sea rose considerably.

Thursday 4th. August: Whilst a skirmish was going on in the rear, the enemy's flagship, with other large vessels, fell upon our royal flagship which was leading the vanguard. They came closer than on the previous day, firing off their heaviest guns from the lowest deck, cutting the trice* of our mainmast and killing some of our soldiers. The enemy's flagship suffered considerable damage and drifted somewhat to the leeward* of our Armada. To windward of us was the enemy's fleet coming up to support their flagship which was in such difficulties that she had to be towed out by eleven long-boats, lowering her standard and firing guns for help. At this moment the wind freshened in favour of the enemy's flagship and we saw that she was getting away from us and had no further need of the shallops* that were towing her out. The enemy was then able to get to windward of us again. When the

Duke saw that further attack was useless and that we were already off the Wight, he fired a signal gun and proceeded on the voyage, followed by the rest of the Armada in good order. The Duke sent Captain Pedro de Leon to Dunkirk to advise the Duke of Parma of our whereabouts and inform him of events, pressing him to come out with all possible speed and join the Armada. At daybreak on Saturday 6th., the fleets were close together and sailed on without exchanging shots until 10 o'clock in the day. The coast of France was sighted, near Boulogne, and we proceeded on our voyage to Calais Roads* where we arrived at 4 o'clock in the afternoon. The Duke was informed by his pilots that if he proceeded any further the currents would force him to run out of the Channel into Norwegian waters. He decided to anchor off Calais, seven leagues* from Dunkirk, where Parma might join him.

This afternoon, the enemy's fleet was reinforced by 36 sail*, including 5 great galleons. This was understood to be John Hawkins's squadron, which had been watching Dunkirk, and the whole of the English fleet now anchored a league distant from our Armada. ..... On Sunday 7th, at daybreak Captain Don Rodrigo Tello arrived from Dunkirk. He reported that the Duke of Parma was at Bruges, where Tello had visited him. Although Parma expressed great joy at the arrival of the Armada, he had not come to Dunkirk up to the night of Saturday 6th, when Tello left there, nor had the embarkation of the men and stores begun. At midnight two fires were seen amongst the English fleet and these two gradually increased to eight. These were eight ships with their sails set, which were drifting with the current directly towards our Armada, all of them burning with great fury. When the Duke saw them approaching and that our men had not diverted them, and fearing that they might contain fire-machines or mines, he ordered the flagship to let go the cables. The rest of the Armada received similar orders, with the instruction that, when the fires had passed, they were to return to the same positions again. The current was so strong that although the flagship and ships near her came to anchor and fired off a signal gun, the other ships of the Armada did not see it and were carried by the current towards Dunkirk.

On Monday 8th the wind freshened from the NW and the English fleet of 136 sail, with wind and tide in its favour, was overhauling us with great speed. The Duke recognized that, if he continued to bear room and tried to come up with the Armada, all would be lost. His Flemish pilots told him that he was already very near the Dunkirk shoals*. In order to save his ships, he decided to face the whole enemy fleet. The enemy's flagship, supported by most of his fleet, attacked our flagship with great fury at daybreak, approaching within musket shot. The attack lasted until 3 in the afternoon, without a moment's cessation of the artillery fire. Nor did our flagship stand away until she had brought the Armada off the sand-banks. The Duke was thus unable to avoid going out of the Channel, nearly all of our stronger ships being so damaged as to be unfit to resist attack, both on account of the cannon fire and their own lack of cannon-balls. The wind from the SSW kept increasing in violence and the Duke continued to go further out to sea, followed by the whole of the enemy's fleet.

On Friday 12th., at dawn, the enemy's fleet was quite close to us, but they saw that we were well together and that the rearguard had been reinforced. The enemy fell astern and sailed towards England until we lost sight of them. Since then we have continued sailing with the same wind until we left the Norwegian Channel. It has been impossible for us to return to the English Channel, even if we desired to do so. We have now, 20th. August, doubled the last of the Scottish Islands to the north and have set our course with a NE wind for Spain.   **Medina Sidonia**

THE EVIDENCE

The Narrator: Alonzo Perez de Guzman, 7th Duke of Medina Sidonia (1550-1615) was son of an aristocratic family of Cadiz which owned estates in that region. King Philip made him Admiral of the Armada because, as highest-ranking Spanish nobleman, he must command complete obedience. Sidonia was modest and courageous, with no qualifications whatever in seamanship, totally dependent upon his advisers. He had no confidence in King Philip's plan for invasion of England. After the Armada's defeat, Sidonia retired to his palace at St. Lucar, but was not dismissed from his naval command. Whilst he was still Admiral, Cadiz was lost in 1596 and Gibraltar in 1606.

The Documents: There is a wealth of published source material, Spanish and English, for the Armada's story. Sidonia's orders "to be observed in the voyage towards England" were published in English in 1888. State Papers relating to our defences were published in 1892-4 and are available in Reference Libraries. They include official despatches, pay and ration scales, letters from Spanish soldiers, lists of ships and equipment and contemporary patriotic ballads. Evidence of captured Spanish sailors was also printed at the time.

CHECK THE EVIDENCE

Are the despatches of a defeated Admiral likely to be the best possible source of information about his campaign? What other evidence would you wish to add.? Find those extra facts in textbooks.

Does the Duke make excuses for the failure of his mission? Does he miss out any essential facts which might discredit him? What reasons did he give for the Armada's failure? What sort of Narrator is he?

The English victory medal was inscribed: *He blew and they were scattered*. Is this a fair description of what Sidonia described? Notice the dangers of both SW and NW winds to the Spanish ships. How much of the English success was due to superior seamanship? How much to the weather? How much to good luck?

INFORMATION

Background to the Armada: The three children of Henry VIII

(1509-47) were Edward VI (1547-53), Mary I (1553-58) and Elizabeth I (1558-1603). Each inherited a different religious policy from the circumstances of their mothers' marriages to Henry VIII. As all three were childless, religious changes followed each succession to the English throne. England was Protestant under Edward, Catholic under Mary, and Protestant again under Elizabeth. Philip of Spain married Mary in 1554, but left her, childless, and returned to Spain. After her death he continued to support the English Catholics' cause. Catholic recusants* were a force to be reckoned with by Elizabeth I's secret service. Many English families sent their sons abroad to be educated by the Jesuits; some returned as secret Catholic priests. They and their families suffered cruel punishments, financially and bodily, during Elizabeth's reign, just as Protestant martyrs died under Queen Mary. Spain's attempt to conquer England by force and the threat of the Inquisition, became the chief rallying-points for Protestant England. The influence of the English Bible, English Prayer Book and Foxe's Book of Martyrs was eventually supreme. The Armada's defeat was Protestant England's first great victory.

The Spanish Armada: better known in Spain as *The Great Enterprise* is well documented, including the reports of secret agents in England. We have seen how English captains were already in conflict with Spain's overseas fleets and how bitterly they resented the punishments of their captured seamen as heretics. Spain's opposition to England came to a head with Elizabeth I's execution of Catholic Mary Queen of Scots in 1587. On 28th. May 1588, a Spanish Armada of 130 ships assembled under command of the Duke of Medina Sidonia, with five squadrons from different regions of Spain. They gathered at Lisbon, harassed by Drake's raiders, awaiting the payment of 1,000,000 golden ducats promised by the Pope. There were 77 Spanish galleons in all, with crews of 6,038 sailors manning 1,736 cannon. The galleons were supported by 23 hulks*, 22 pataches*, 4 galleys* and 4 galleasses* from Naples. The latter, better suited to Mediterranean waters, were rowed by 2,000 oarsmen. Each ship carried 200-300 soldiers, recruited all over Catholic Europe. Sidonia complained bitterly about the low standard of these troops, some "so useless that they were no good, even as pioneers ... absolutely unserviceable old men."

The Spaniards' rations were 2lb of fresh bread or 1 lb of hard biscuit* daily, with 1 pint of sherry or 1 pint of wine. On Sundays and Thursdays each man received 6oz of bacon and 2oz of rice; on Mondays and Wednesdays, 6oz of cheese and 3oz of beans or peas; on Wednesdays, Fridays and Saturdays there was an issue of 6oz of fish per man, also with beans or peas. Each man also received 1 oz of oil and vinegar on fish-days. The water ration was restricted to 3 pints per man a day.

The English fleet's Lord High Admiral was **Charles Howard, Lord Effingham (1536-1624)**, who succeeded his father the Duke of Norfolk as Admiral. Howard was a suspected Catholic. He commanded the English fleet from his flagship *Ark Royal* and his *regiment* comprised 22 ships and 3,868 men. The other Captain and Admiral was Sir Francis Drake, with 30 ships and 2,737 mariners, gunners and soldiers. English captains were paid 2s.6d. (12 p) a day and the total cost of wages and supplies for the fleet was £19,228. English sea-rations, for two meals a day were: 1lb of biscuit, 1 gallon of beer per man and 2lb of salt beef or bacon, with 1 pint of peas. Fish days, even in a Protestant Navy, being cheaper, accounted for 20 meals a month, on Wednesdays, Fridays and Saturdays. A Spanish agent reported that Drake was "extremely negligent in guarding his ships; 1,000 of his men have mutinied for want of pay." The English ships also suffered from disease. By August, "the infection is grown very great; they sicken one day and die the next." This was thought to be the plague, and many ships had hardly enough men to weigh their anchors. Fortunately, as our story tells us, the Armada was already in flight by then.

The intention had been to embark the Duke of Parma's army from the Netherlands, then to sail up the Thames estuary, to invade

England. The running fight up the Channel lasted 11 days and the two Dukes were never able to get together. Driven from their refuge in the Calais Roads and heavily defeated off Gravelines, the Spaniards fell foul of strong SW winds, driving them around northern Scotland and western Ireland. Though the English fleet abandoned the chase through shortage of gunpowder, rough weather accounted for many of the surviving ships. The English captains complained bitterly, in a despatch to the Privy Council, that "if our wants of victuals and munitions were supplied, we would pursue them to the furthest that they durst have gone." Otherwise, they said, we must call off their pursuit and defend our own coast. By the time the surviving Spanish ships limped home in October, some had sailed 5,000 miles. Only 65 ships returned to Spain, but not one English ship was lost. The English advantage, as in the Battle of Britain in 1940, lay in their closeness to their home base, and the manoeuvrability of their small fighters. The Spanish Armada's defeat ensured the success of Protestant rebels in the Netherlands and gave Elizabethan England a vigorous sense of national identity.

WHAT IS YOUR VERDICT?

We shall often ask: "Does History repeat itself?" Certainly there is a similarity between the Armada's defeat and that of the German Luftwaffe during the Battle of Britain in 1940. What would have been the long-term effects of a victory in either case?

Both countries, Spain and England advertised God's support of their cause. In the same way, the Germans in 1914 used the slogan *God with us*. England too has often claimed a righteous advantage for her Christian soldiers. What do you think about these claims? How much right did the Spaniards have on their side in their attempted invasion of England?

On the other hand, was England the completely innocent victim of the Spanish attack? If so, does an innocent nation, attacked by a stronger power, have a greater right to claim divine support?

GUNPOWDER, TREASON AND PLOT!

After Queen Elizabeth died in 1603, her cousin, the King of Scotland, James VI, became the first Stuart king of England as James I. He was unpopular, especially with his outlawed Catholic subjects. They plotted to blow up the King in Parliament and start a Catholic rebellion in the Midlands. Their plot was discovered, or betrayed, and the hit man, Guy Fawkes, was arrested on November 4th. 1605. As so often happens with suspected terrorists, he was persuaded to confess. His confession and those of his friends who had not died resisting arrest are found with other original 17th. century papers in the Public Record Office in London. Here are some brief extracts from their first-hand story. Our text is selective and abridged; some words and phrases have been modernised.

From Guy Fawkes's Confession: First, they hired the house at Westminster from a man called Ferris. Having found the house, they then set out to make a mine under the Upper House* of Parliament. They began digging the mine about December 11th. (1604). Five of them began the work and soon after, they took another man in with them, having first sworn him, on the Sacrament, to secrecy. When they came to the wall, which was about three yards thick, and found it a matter of great difficulty, they took on another man in the same way. All seven were gentlemen. Having worked up to the wall before Christmas, they ceased until after the holiday. The day before Christmas, having a mass of earth that came out of the mine, they took it to the garden of the house.

After Christmas, they worked at the wall until February and worked halfway through the wall. All the time that the others worked, he stood as sentinel, watching for any man who came near. If anyone came near the place, they ceased digging until he gave them notice to start again. All seven of them stayed in the

GUNPOWDER, TREASON AND PLOT!

TRANSCRIPT of an EXTRACT
(Final paragraph and signature)
from GUY FAWKES'S CONFESSION

He also saith he did not intend to set fier to the Tr(ain until)
the Kinge was come into the howse, and then he purposed
to do it with a peece of touch wood, and with a matche,
also (which were aboute him when he was apprehended on the
4 day of Nov: last at 11 of the clocke at night)
that the powder might more surely take fier a quarter
of an hower after.
            Guido Faukes
Taken before us
(Ed) Coke
W Waad
Edward Forsett

TRANSCRIPT OF A LETTER FROM
FRANCIS TRESHAM (one of the plotters)
To His BROTHER-IN-LAW, LORD MONTEAGLE
           26th OCTOBER 1605

My lord, out of the love I bear to some of your friends, I have a
care of your preservation. Therefore I would advise you, as you
tender your life, to devise some excuse to shift of your attendance
at this Parliament. For God and man hath concurred to punish the
wickedness of this time.

And think not slightly of this advertisement but retire yourself
into your country, where you may expect the event in safety. For
though there be no appeaance of any stir, yet I say they shall
receive a terrible blow this Parliament - and yet they shall not see
who hurts them.

This counsel is not to be condemned - because it may do you
good, and can do you no harm. For the danger is past as soon as
you have burnt this letter. And I hope God will give you the grace
to make good use of it, to whose holy protection I commend you.

house and had shot and gunpowder. They were resolved to die in that place before they would surrender or be captured.

As they were working, they heard a rushing noise in the cellar, caused by Bright selling his coal. Then this examinant, fearing that they had been discovered, went into the cellar and viewed it and saw that it was more useful for their purpose. Understanding that it was to let, his master, Mr. Percy hired the cellar for a year at £4 rent. After Christmas, 20 barrels of gunpowder were brought by them to a house which they had on the Bankside. From that house they removed the powder into the cellar and covered it with faggots* which they had laid in the cellar earlier. He says that he did not intend to set fire to the fuse until the King had come into the House, then he intended to light it with a piece of touchwood* and with a match*. These were on his person when he was arrested on the fourth day of November last, at 11 o'clock at night. The powder was on a 15 minute fuse.

From Thomas Winter's Confession: Not out of hope of obtaining pardon for confessing, but only at your Honour's command, I will briefly set down my own confession, since I see that such actions are not pleasing to Almighty God - and everything, or most of it, has been confessed already.

I remained with my brother in the country for All Saints' Day 1603, about which time Mr. Catesby sent there, entreating me to come to London. He said that he had bethought himself of a way at one and the same time to deliver us from all our troubles and - without any foreign help - to replant the Catholic religion again. He told me, in other words, that his plan was to blow up the Parliament House with gunpowder. For, he said, it is in that place that they have done us all the mischief, so perhaps God hath designed that place for their punishment.

At Easter, up came Mr. Thomas Percy. The first words he spoke were: "Shall we always, gentlemen, talk and never do anything?"

GUNPOWDER, TREASON AND PLOT!

Mr. Catesby took him aside and spoke to him about what could be done, if we all first took an oath of secrecy. This we decided to do in about two or three days' time. So we met behind St. Clement's: Mr. Catesby, Mr. Percy, Mr. Wright, Mr. Guy Fawkes and myself. We took each others' oath of secrecy upon a Prayer Book, in a room where there was no-one else. Then Mr. Catesby disclosed his secret to Mr. Percy, whilst Jack Wright and I told Mr. Fawkes and they both approved.

Then Mr. Percy sent to take the house which Mr. Catesby, in my absence, had discovered belonged to a Mr. Ferris. With some difficulty he obtained it and became - as Ferris was before him - a tenant of Mr. Wynniard. Mr. Fawkes took the name of Mr. Percy's servant, calling himself Johnson, because his face was almost unknown, and received the keys of the house. It was thought convenient to hire a house near Mr. Percy's. There we might keep a store of powder and wood for the mine. Once this was ready we would take it by night to the other house near Parliament, because we were unwilling to reveal that by often going in and out.

A fortnight before Christmas, Mr. Percy and Mr. Wright came to London. We had provided a good part of the gunpowder, so we, all five, entered with tools fit to begin our work. We provided ourselves with baked meats, the less to need sending out for. We went in late at night and were never seen - except for Mr. Percy's man. At that time we were working under a little entry, to the wall of the Parliament House. We under-propped it as we went, with wood. About Candlemas* we brought the powder which we had stored at Lambeth over in a boat and laid it in Mr. Percy's house, because we were unwilling to have all our danger in one place. We worked another fortnight in the mine, against the stone wall, which was very hard to get through. At that time we called in Kit Wright. About Easter, we found an opportunity to rent the cellar, so we decided to store the powder and leave the mine.

GUNPOWDER, TREASON AND PLOT!

After this, Mr. Fawkes laid into the cellar 1,000 sticks and 500 faggots. He covered up the powder with that, so that we could leave the house open to let anyone come in who wished to. Meanwhile, Mr. Fawkes and I brought in some new powder, suspecting the first lot to be damp. We took it to the cellar and set it in order. Then Parliament was prorogued* until November 5th., so we all went away until some 10 days before that. Two days later, it being Sunday, October 26th, at night, someone came to my room and told me that a letter had been given to my Lord Monteagle, to this effect: That he wished his Lordship's absence from the Parliament, because a blow would there be given.

I went on the morrow to Mr. Webb's and told this to Mr. Catesby, assuring him that the matter was discovered and begging him to leave the country. He told me that he would see it further yet and decided to send Mr. Fawkes to try the uttermost. On Friday 1st. November, Mr. Catesby, Mr. Tresham and I met at Barnet, where we questioned how this letter had been sent to Lord Monteagle. We could not imagine how, for Mr. Tresham - our only suspect - denied it. About five o'clock, on Tuesday 5th. November, I went down towards the Parliament House and, being in the middle of King Street, found the guard standing by. He would not let me pass, and, as I returned, I heard one say: "There is a treason discovered, in which the King and the Lords shall have been blown up!" Then I was fully convinced that all was known. I went to the stable where my horse was kept, and rode into the country.

On Thursday, we took armour at my Lord Windsor's, and went that night to a Stephen Lyttleton's house at Holbeach. There I found Mr. Catesby reasonably well, Mr. Percy, both the Wrights, Mr. Rookwood and Mr. Grant. I asked them what they meant to do. They answered: "We mean to die here!" I said that I would do as they did. At 11 o'clock in the morning, the Sheriff of Worcester's men came to attack the house. As I walked into the courtyard, I was shot in the shoulder, which lost me the use of my arm. The next shot killed the elder Mr. Wright, after him the younger Mr. Wright and fourthly Ambrose Rookwood.

Then said Mr. Catesby: "Stand by Tom, and we'll die together!"

"Sir," quoth I, "I have lost the use of my right arm and fear that this will cause me to be taken."

So, as we stood close together, Mr. Catesby, Mr. Percy and myself, those two were shot, as far as I could guess with one bullet. Then the company entered upon me and hurt me in the belly with a Pike, and gave me other wounds.

THE EVIDENCE

The Narrators: Guy Fawkes, alias Guido Faukes or Faulx (1570-1605): was born a Protestant at York. He later became a Catholic and served in the Spanish army in the Netherlands. Invited to return to England by Catesby, he was the only professional terrorist of the Powder Treason . Notice too, that he was the only member of the gang caught red-handed, as the others, like Winter, had fled cross-country. The King ordered that: "If he will not otherwise confess, the gentler tortures are to be first used unto him, and then, by degrees to the uttermost pain." The gaolers said that Fawkes confessed as soon as he saw the rack, and it was not used. When he was hanged in January, a spectator said that: "His body being weak with torture and sickness, he was scarce able to get up the ladder".

Thomas Winter: brother of Robert Winter, another plotter, was born in Worcestershire and related to Robert Catesby and Francis Tresham. Winter was secretary to Lord Monteagle and Tresham was Monteagle's brother-in-law. They were all Catholics, and Monteagle, Tresham and Catesby had already been involved in the Earl of Essex's rebellion against Queen Elizabeth in 1601. Winter travelled abroad with messages to Catholic priests and English exiles. He reported his meeting with Guy Fawkes and recruited him as a brave and obedient soldier. Catesby came from an unlucky family; his ancestor, Richard Catesby was a supporter of

Richard III, hanged by Henry Tudor after the Battle of Bosworth in 1485. Winter was hanged, drawn and quartered after a brief trial in 1606.

CHECK THE EVIDENCE

Read the transcript of Monteagle's letter. Is there anything suspicious about this warning?

Are confessions taken under torture likely to be reliable evidence? Notice how the writer takes down answers to one question after another, but puts all the answers together, to make it look as if the prisoner spoke the evidence as one continuous statement. The witness writes nothing but his signature. Practise this with your friends (no torture!) and see whether it can affect their statements. As to whether the accused were tortured or not, look at the facsimile of Guy Fawkes's confession and his signature (Picture Pack No. TT3/10). This is not his normal handwriting. Why is it so infirmly written?

Do the two confessions match in every detail? Is it more or less suspicious if they do? Several copies have been found with the original transcripts. These show that some lines were or left out in the fair copies. What do you think of this sort of evidence? Is it likely to happen in the writing-up of any statement?

The dubious nature of the confessions - as often happens today - draws our attention away from the more circumstantial evidence. Confession or not, there seems to be no doubt that Guy Fawkes was arrested under the House of Lords, by a half-dug mine, with a quantity of gunpowder and a fuse. How much more evidence did they need? Why did they need to torture the suspects if the other evidence was obvious enough? Now find out about the flaws and dangers in the ready acceptance of circumstantial evidence. (*Rumpole of the Bailey,* written by a lawyer, is very good on this subject.)

GUNPOWDER, TREASON AND PLOT!

INFORMATION

King James I (1603-25): was first of the Stuart kings. He was the son of Mary, Queen of Scots, who had been executed by order of Elizabeth I and grandson of Elizabeth's cousin, James V. He had been James VI of Scotland since he was a baby in 1567. He inherited many problems from the Tudor Queen and made most of them worse. He was described as the wisest fool in Christendom, and was certainly a thoroughly unpleasant person. He depended on several homosexual favourites and his own judgment was erratic. His father had been murdered by a bomb and James was terrified that he too would be assassinated. As king of Scotland he had already been the victim of treasonable plots.

King James had promised to settle England's religious problems but, like Elizabeth I's, his laws prevented Catholics from practising their religion in England and punished priests who hid in the great houses. Fear of foreign invasion hardened ordinary folks' opposition to Catholic neighbours; Winter denied seeking any foreign assistance for the plot. Catholics were strong in Worcestershire, Warwickshire and the far North of England, where several of the plotters' families lived. James's minister who had managed his succession to the throne was Robert Cecil, son of Queen Elizabeth's old Treasurer. His spies, like MI5 and MI6, worked at home and abroad.

In the first year of his reign, the King managed to alienate both extremes of religious belief. At the Hampton Court Conference he insulted the Puritans (who would later defeat his son), offering no concessions; at the same time Catholic priests were ordered out of the country. The King also began an endless dispute with Parliament over taxation and Royal extravagance. These were the seeds of inevitable Civil War and in 1605 a group of Catholic dissidents decided to take decisive action. The failure of their plot gave James an advantage over at least one section of the opposition to his High Church policy.

GUNPOWDER, TREASON AND PLOT!

WHAT IS YOUR VERDICT?

James I's instructions about torture were not openly stated, but they tell us a great deal about Tudor and Stuart government. We hear more today about tyrannous regimes which are known to have used brutal methods of interrogation. Some of these are as blatant about torture as James I. Do we turn blind eyes on injustices we take for granted?

Cecil's spies were keeping their eye on the Gunpowder Plot from the beginning. Is it possible that they helped the plot to continue, so that the English Catholics would be blamed, disgraced and never forgiven? Some writers have suggested that the plotters were double agents, turned at the time of the Essex Plot and deliberately sacrificed to frighten the King in 1605. Could there be any truth in these rumours? Who wrote the unsigned letter to Lord Monteagle? He received it on October 26th, but the conspirators were not arrested until November 4th. Why was there this delay?

Was the Gunpowder Plot a fair attempt to change English religious laws, or merely criminal terrorism? If a rebel group of dissidents decides that there is no other way to achieve their rights than terrorism, is this acceptable as a normal historical pattern?

What is your verdict on Guy Fawkes and his friends? - brave or stupid? - vicious or heroic? - innocent or guilty? Were they set up or framed?

Why do we still celebrate Bonfire Night after more than 300 years?

The most famous Elizabethan courtier was Sir Walter Raleigh. We do not know whether the story of the sacrifice of his cloak is true (perhaps children could set about finding out?). The written evidence for our own story is authentic - or at least is taken from original sources.

Look first at the picture of two boys listening to the yarns of an Elizabethan seaman. Think about the prospects which the future might hold, in 16th century Devon, for such a boy. Then read the end of the story, as Raleigh's son told it, 33 years after his father's execution for treason. Our story takes the form of a petition which he put to the Roundhead Parliament, in 1651, two years after the execution of James I's own son.

Like the Victorian painter of *The Boyhood of Raleigh,* we must be prepared to use our imaginations. This is the sad story of one lifetime, from boyhood enthusiasm to the violent death of an elderly man. There were many disappointments and failures along the way, but a great deal of glory too. Let us begin with Millais's pictorial legend of his otherwise unrecorded boyhood, then see what friends, enemies and Princes did to make his dreams come true - or disappear.

When King James came to England, he found Sir Walter Raleigh (by favour of his late Mistress, Queen Elizabeth), Lord Warden of the Stannaries*, Lord Lieutenant of Devon and Cornwall, Captain of the Guard and Governor of the Island of Jersey, with a large possession of lands, both in England and Ireland.

The King, for some weeks, used him with great kindness, and was pleased to acknowledge several presents which he had received from Raleigh, when he was still in Scotland, for which he gave him thanks. But, finding him, (as he said) a martial* man, addicted to foreign affairs and great actions, he feared lest he might engage England in a war abroad (a thing most hated and contrary to the

SIR WALTER RALEIGH

King's nature.) Therefore, the King began to look upon him with a jealous eye, especially after Raleigh presented him with a book in which, with clever arguments, he opposed England's peace with Spain, which was then coming to a treaty. He persuaded the King instead to continue war with that Prince, promising (and that with great probability), that within a few years he would reduce the West Indies to the King's obedience.

Sir Walter's enemies soon discovered the King's temper*, and resolved* at once to rid him of this troublesome man, and to enrich themselves with Sir Walter's lands and offices. They plotted to accuse him and Lord Cobham, (a simple man, of very noble birth and great possessions) of high treason. The particulars of their accusation I am utterly ignorant of (as, I think, everyone else is, both then and now). I find that, in general terms, Raleigh and Cobham were accused of plotting with Spain to bring in a foreign army, and to proclaim the Infanta* of Spain as Queen of England. This accusation was made without any proof, the whole thing was as ridiculous as possible. Raleigh was condemned without any witnesses being brought against him. They pretended that Lord Cobham had accused him in a letter, but in another letter to Sir Walter, Cobham, after his own acquittal, cleared him of all treason, either against the king or the state. That original letter is in my hands, and can be produced at any time.

Upon Raleigh's condemnation, all his lands and offices were seized, and he was committed, a close prisoner, to the Tower. They found that his Castle of Sherborne and its lands had, for a long time, been entailed* on his children, so that he could not be made to forfeit them during his lifetime. For seven years after his imprisonment, he kept Sherborne. Then it appeared that Mr. Robert Carr, a young Scottish gentleman grew in great favour with the King. Having no fortune of his own, they decided to lay the foundation of his fortune upon the ruin of Sir Walter Raleigh. They challenged the transfer of Sherborne in the Exchequer Court, where, for want of a single word in the documents (which was found in the book-copy and was only a clerk's misprint), they declared the covenant invalid* and Sherborne forfeit to the Crown. This judgement could be easily foreseen without witch-craft, since Raleigh's chief judge was his greatest enemy and the case was argued between a penniless prisoner and the King of England. Thus was Sherborne given to Sir Robert Carr, afterwards Earl of Somerset.

The Lady Raleigh, with her children, humbly and earnestly begged the King for pity, on her knees, but could only get the answer: "He mun* have the land, he mun have it for Carr." She, although she was a woman of very high spirit and noble birth, fell down on her knees, with her hands raised to Heaven, beseeching God Almighty to look upon the justice of her cause and to punish those who had ruined her and her poor children. What has happened to that Royal Family since then is too sad and disastrous for me to repeat, but it is there for all to see.

Sir Walter, being of vigorous constitution and perfect health, had now worn out 16 years imprisonment and had seen the disastrous end to all his enemies. New persons and new interests springing up at court, he found reasons to obtain his liberty on condition of going on a voyage to Guiana for the discovery of a gold mine. That unhappy voyage is already known to all men. He was betrayed from the very start, his letters and plans being secretly sent to the Spanish Ambassador. Whereby, he found such strong opposition upon that place that, though he took and fired* the town of St. Thoma, yet he lost his eldest son in that service, and being desperately sick himself, lost all his hopes.

Immediately upon his return home, he was made prisoner, and by the violent attack of the Spanish Ambassador and others who could not think their estates safe whilst Raleigh's head was on his shoulders, the King resolved to take advantage of his former condemnation 16 years before. This was because he could not find any reason to take his life for any more recent activities. The

King had given Raleigh a Commission under the Great Seal to execute martial law on his own soldiers. This was considered by the best lawyers to be a full pardon for any offence before that time. Without any further trouble at law, they cut off his head. So, Sir Walter was condemned for being a friend to the Spaniards and lost his life for attacking them!

THE EVIDENCE

The Painter: **Sir John Everett Millais (1829-96)** was born at Southampton and studied art at the Royal Academy schools, exhibiting his first picture when he was only seventeen. He was influenced by the pre-Raphaelites (See *CLASSROOM GALLERY*) and painted *The Boyhood of Raleigh* in 1870. The future poet and explorer sits in rapt attention, listening to an old sailor telling stories of the sea. We can imagine the thoughts and visions which fill the boys' imagination. Notice the discarded model ship in the foreground.

The Narrator: **Carew Raleigh** was Sir Walter's younger, surviving son. After his father's disgrace, he attended the royal Court, but was advised to leave and travel abroad because his appearance was like the ghost of his father to King James I. Carr was made Earl of Somerset but was disgraced and imprisoned in 1616 - the disastrous end to Raleigh's enemies which is mentioned in the petition. Carew took no part in the Civil War, but returned to petition the Commonwealth Parliament for the restoration of his family home.

The Documents: Carew's petition and many other documents about Raleigh's life are found in a family collection of papers printed as *The Somers Tracts* in 1809. These papers include the very moving farewell letter from Raleigh to his wife, Bess, written on the night before his execution, which is carefully described. The printed *State Papers Domestic* for the reigns of Elizabeth and James I also have many references to Raleigh. Details of the five voyages to Virginia, and Raleigh's first attempt to plant a colony there, are very fully described by the colonists in *Hakluyt's book of Voyages.*

Victorian narrative painters: The Victorians took a romantic view of English History; their favourite books were historical novels, like those of Walter Scott. They painted historical characters in dramatic situations and fancy dress. These pictures are full of almost photographic details and bright colour. The painters saw History as the good old days of Merry England. They portrayed romances, of ancient British heroes like Boadicea and Caractacus and Anglo-Saxon kings like Alfred and Harold. Victorian story-tellers believed in a legend of Saxon freedom, overcome for a time, in spite of heroic resistance, by Norman conquerors, strong medieval kings and wicked barons. Freedom was restored by Parliament as the Victorians knew it. Tyrannous Kings, however noble, were over-ruled, defeated and killed by the people. This was tragic, but necessary. Their medieval subjects were the Crusaders, Edward III, the Black Prince and Henry V, knights in armour and damsels in distress.

The Tudor and Elizabethan periods were also popular. Stories of young girls or innocent children - the Princes in the Tower and Charles I's children - all were painted to tell a story which would touch our hearts. Delaroche's *Lady Jane Grey,* 17 years old and Queen for only nine days, kneels blindfolded on the scaffold, within minutes of the axe, bravely groping for the block with a hesitant hand. It is fashionable nowadays to dismiss these unashamedly sentimental pictures, condemning the Victorians for a false view of History. We must be careful; the original Tudor documents of Lady Jane's execution, for example, tell the identical story of a courageous, innocent death. What the paintings cannot describe are the motives of earlier people for their actions.

Millais, who painted *The Boyhood of Raleigh* also gives us yet another version of The Princes in the Tower in 1878, another Civil War drama in *The Proscribed Royalist* (1853) and the more unusual subject of *Princess Elizabeth in Prison at St. James's* (1879). These and many more Victorian narrative paintings are explained and illustrated by Roy Strong in his book: *And when did you last see your father? : The Victorian Painter and British History* (1978)

CHECK THE EVIDENCE

What evidence did the the painter have for the subject of his picture? Is it a likely scene?

Carew's petition is another source which is quite certain to be prejudiced. Does this seem to have affected the reported facts at all? These can be checked in most textbooks. Does it matter very much if a story teller is known to be biased? What difference will it make if another writer is biased, but we have no way of knowing this?

Our story does not tell you whether Raleigh's family were successful in regaining their property at Sherborne in Dorset. How would you set about finding out if they were or not?

INFORMATION

Sir Walter Raleigh (1552-1618): was born in a Devon manor house, at Hayes Barton, near Sidmouth. Educated at Oriel College, Oxford, his career began as a soldier of 17, amongst a troop of 100 gentleman volunteers serving the Protestant cause for 6 years in France. His half-brother, Sir Humphrey Gilbert was granted lands in North America and Raleigh joined him in an unsuccessful expedition to Newfoundland. He returned to help put down rebellion in Ireland with his own troop of 100 men. This daring service brought him to court as a friend of the Earl of

Leicester, whom he accompanied to the Netherlands. The ageing Queen heaped favours on her young courtier. He was appointed Captain of the Guard and General at sea, was given monopolies in trade of wine and broadcloth, and became Lord Warden of the Stannaries*, Lord Lieutenant of Cornwall and later, governor of Jersey. He was knighted in 1584 and in the next year Devonshire elected him their MP. As Vice-admiral of Devon and Cornwall he raised the militia against the Armada and commanded a squadron of volunteers.

Between 1584 and 1590 five separate voyages were made to North America to establish a colony named Virginia, on the coast, at 360. These were made chiefly *at the charges of the honourable Sir Walter Raleigh, Knight,* by a grant of royal letters patent* in his favour. In 1585 a colony of 108 men was planted* under the leadership of Master Ralf Lane, to remain one full year in Virginia. A second colony of 91 men, 17 women and 9 children were transported in 3 ships in 1587. John White was appointed Governor and a town named Raleigh was established. Two children, Virginia Dare and Harvey (no other name) were born there. White complained bitterly that furniture and other necessities ordered by Raleigh were never transported and there was dissatisfaction amongst the colonists, who missed their dainty food and soft feather-beds. This was the first permanent settlement to be made in North America. Amongst its chief commodities were tobacco and potatoes. Raleigh's original settlement was not a success, but Jamestown was founded in 1607 and a regular governor and council was set up for its government.

Raleigh lost the Queen's favour in 1592, because she was jealous of his love affair with her lady-in-waiting Bess Throckmorton, daughter of a leading Catholic family. For this, he spent some time in the Tower and was forbidden the Court for four years. He married Bess and lived peacefully at Sherborne for a time, but became obsessed with the vision of Guiana and, in 1595 sailed up the Orinoco with 5 ships. He published *The History of Guiana.*

On James's accession, Raleigh was dismissed from court and accused of plotting with Cobham, as his son described. He was sentenced to death, but was pardoned on the scaffold and spent 12 years imprisoned in the Tower. There he wrote a *History of the World* which was suppressed as being "too saucy" in its criticism of Kings. In 1616 he was released to undertake an expedition to Guiana in search of gold. These plans were betrayed to the Spaniards, who attacked him on the Orinoco. Raleigh and his men were stricken with sickness, his eldest, favourite son was killed and Raleigh returned, alone in the *Destiny,* without having discovered any gold mine. He wrote an Apology for the failure of his mission, but was executed in 1618, on the original, 15-year-old charge of supporting Spain. James I, grovelling, declared that he would punish anyone who, like Raleigh, carried out any acts of violence against his dear brother of Spain.

The Stuart Succession: was never secure. From the end of Elizabeth's reign, and after James I's accession, the chief contender was the *Infanta* of Spain, whose claims could be traced from John of Gaunt, ancestor of the medieval Lancastrians and their Tudor heirs. Robert Cecil, Elizabeth's chief minister was rumoured, falsely, to support the Infanta. Aware of the Spanish claim, James wooed the English Catholics with false promises and sent cringing letters to the Pope. In 1601, part of Essex's plot, for which he was executed, opposed Cecil and Raleigh, accusing them of supporting the Spanish claim.

Another contender for the succession who implicated Raleigh was James's cousin, Arabella Stuart, whom Elizabeth had sometimes favoured. Her claim descended from Henry VII's daughter Margaret and she enjoyed the popular advantage of having been born in England. Several plots were made in her favour, but in 1615 she died in the Tower. Raleigh's downfall was the result of James's insecurity.

A COURTIER'S DOWNFALL

WHAT IS YOUR VERDICT?

You saw an earlier reaction against King James I in our last story. What sort of picture are you beginning to get of this Scottish king?

You might call King James a coward, for wanting peace, and consider Raleigh as a hero, for facing England's enemies gallantly. On the other hand, you might think that James's peaceable nature was that of a sensible man, and Raleigh's reistance to Spain that of a chauvinist bully-boy. What do you think?

Another courtier of James I's son, Charles I, went to the block, quoting the Prayer Book: "Put not your faith in Princes!" The Stuarts have this unfortunate reputation for untrustworthiness. Find out more about their actions and make a list of any other broken promises. Or another list of royalist friends and supporters loyally protected from the Kings' enemies.

Make a list of all those ventures which Raleigh organized, which failed for one reason or another. Was he just another failure, making excuses for everything he did wrongly? Or was he a man of genius, defeated by lesser men?

Often in History, we are tempted to say that there is no smoke without fire. Do you suspect that Raleigh was not entirely in the right and James I not entirely in the wrong in the story which Raleigh's son tells us? Explain your reasons for this suspicion.

Raleigh was 66 years old when he died. In England today, he would just have become an old-age pensioner. Find modern examples of pensioners who are still living adventurous lives.

Writers - contemporary and modern - often accuse, or drop hints that a man, like King James I was homosexual. Should this affect our view of his character? More important, would it have affected the opinion of people of that day? How did this view of James I affect Sir Walter Raleigh and his son, for example?

LADY BRILLIANA DEFENDS HER CASTLE

In July 1642, Parliament raised an army to fight King Charles I. The King called on the county militias* to support him, but Parliament had already passed a *Militia Bill* of its own. The King raised his standard in Nottingham, defended by 8 regiments of cavalry and 16 infantry battalions. Parliament's Captain General, the Earl of Essex mustered 1,600 soldiers and the King retreated westward to Chester, hoping for Royalist Welsh support. In September, the King's nephew, Prince Rupert, advancing to meet the King, drove off a Roundhead force near Worcester, but decided to abandon the city. The Civil War had begun in the same fields where it would end, nine years later.

In the depths of Herefordshire, Lady Brilliana Harley kept an anxious watch on the situation, from her family's small castle at Brampton Bryan. Her husband Sir Robert, a determined enemy of the King, was busy in London, organizing Parliament's resistance. Although Brilliana heard that Essex's men had seized the City of Hereford, most of the county gentry, many of the ordinary towns-folk and villagers too, were strongly Royalist. The Harleys were not popular with their neighbours. Surrounded by enemies, who might strike at any time, she wrote urgent despatches to her husband, enclosing anxious letters to her eldest son, Edward, at Oxford. Here are extracts from some of those letters, telling the story of Brampton's siege.

17th July, 1642, For my dear son, Mr. Edward Harley: By the enclosed paper to your father you will know how poor Herefordshire is affected. But, dear Ned, I hope that you and I will remember for whose cause we are hated. It is for the cause of our God, and I am confident that the Lord will save us.

I sent Mr. Samuel to Hereford to spy out their behaviour. He tells me that all in the City cry out against your father. My dear Ned, I cannot think that I am safe at Brampton, but by no means would I have you come here. I trust the Lord will tell your father what is best and I don't doubt that we shall pray for one another.

I wish that my cousin Adams was out of this house, for I am sure that he will give the other side whatever help he can. Tell your father so, for he does not know what plans they have in Herefordshire, nor which way they will go. The Captain of the Volunteers is a man called Barrell. He was a tradesman, and once was Mayor of Hereford.

July 19th: I long to see you but would not have you come down here, for I cannot believe that this country* is safe for you. By the papers I have sent your father you will understand the temper of it. I hope that your father will give me full instructions how I may best have my house guarded, if need be. My dear Ned, I thank God that I am not afraid. It is the Lord's cause we have stood for.

Even if I had not needed to send to your father, I would still have sent this messenger-boy to London. He is such a rogue that I dare not keep him in my house, and I dare not let him go out into the country, lest he join with the company of Royalist volunteers or some other such crew. I have given him no more money than enough to pay his way up to London. Because I want him to make haste and be sure to go to London, I have told him that you will give him more if he comes to you in good time and doesn't loiter. I have enclosed half a crown*. Give him what you think fit and tell him not to come back here. Persuade him to go to sea, or some other sort of work. He thinks he is coming back again.

My cousin Davis tells me that no-one can make lead shot but those whose trade it is, so I have made our plumber write to Worcester for half a hundredweight* of shot. I sent to Worcester because I didn't want it known round here. If your father thinks that this is not enough, I will send for more.

July 2nd: My dear Ned, when I first saw how outrageously this county aroused themselves against your father, my anger was so great, and my sorrow too, that I hardly had the patience to stay here. But now, I have considered it carefully, that if I go away, I shall leave all your father owns to be the prey of our enemies, which they would be very glad of. So, if it please God, I intend to stay as long as possible, if I live. That is my decision, unless your father forbids it. I cannot make a better use of my life, next to serving my God, than to do what good I can for you.

December 13th: My dear Ned - My heart has known no rest since you went. I confess I was never so full of sorrow. I am afraid that our supply of corn and malt will not hold out, if this war continues. They say that they will burn our barns and I am afraid that they will place soldiers so near me that there will be no way out. My comfort is that you are not with me here, lest they should capture you. But I do most dearly miss you. I wish, if it pleased God, that I could be with your father. I would have written to him, but I dare not write on paper. Dear Ned, please write to me, but write secretly on a piece of cloth, as this letter is. There are 1,000 dragoons* come into Hereford.

December 25th: I pray that you discuss with your father whether he thinks it best that I should send away most of the serving-men that are in this house, and whether it is best for me to leave Brampton, or by God's help to hold out. I will be willing to do whatever he would have me do. I was never in such sorrows as I have been since you left me. I hope that the Lord will deliver me, but they are most cruelly set against me.

January 28th, 1643: My dear Ned, I know that it will grieve you to know how badly I am treated. It is with as much malice as can be. Mr. Wigmore will not let the fowler* bring me any poultry, nor will he let any of my servants pass. They have forbidden our tenants to pay their rents. They have driven off our young horses to Wigmore and none of my servants dare go as far as that town.

If God were not merciful to me, I would be in a very miserable condition. They threaten every day to besiege me with soldiers. My hope is that they do not capture me, for surely they would use me cruelly. I am told that they intend to leave your father neither root nor branch. You and I must forgive them, ask for the prayers of the godly for us at Brampton.

February 14th: Nine days ago my Lord Herbert was at Hereford where he stayed a week. They held a council of war on the best way to take Brampton. They decided to blow it up, a plan which pleased them all. The Sheriff of Radnorshire, with the trained bands of his county and some of the Herefordshire soldiers were ordered to come against me. The soldiers came to Presteigne, but it pleased God to call my Lord Herbert away to oppose our supporters in the Forest of Dean. Now, they say, they will starve me out of my house. They have taken away all your father's rents and say that they will drive off the cattle and then I shall have nothing to live on. Their whole aim is to force me to let what men I have go, so that they can set upon my house and order a few rogues to cut our throats, so that they can say they didn't know who did it. They tell me that I shall be safe, but I have no reason to trust them.

March 8th: My dear Ned - I would have been very glad to have received a letter from you by Mr. Taylor. Dear Ned, find some way to write to me, so that I may know how the world goes and how it is with your father and yourself. It is death to be amongst so many enemies and not to hear from those I love so dearly.

I have sent you a copy of a summons which was sent me, that if I do not give them my house and whatever they want, I shall be prosecuted as a traitor. I wish your father would think seriously on what I should do, whether to stay at Brampton or move to some other place. I hear that there are 600 soldiers raised to come against me.

6th. May: To my grief, I must tell you that honest Petter is taken. Six men set upon him, three shot at him as he was opening a gate not far from Mortimers Cross. He fought valiantly with them and wounded two of them. If there had not been 6 against him he would have escaped. He was wounded in the head and shoulder, but not fatally. He is in prison in Ludlow. I have done all that is possible to get him out, but it cannot be done. I have found him very faithful to me, and he wanted to come and join you.

June 11th: I heard from Gloucester, last Thursday by someone I sent to find out news. Sir William Waller went on Tuesday towards the west and Lieutenant-colonel Massey is ordered to be Governor of Gloucester. I am very grateful to Colonel Massey, please tell your father so and ask him to give Massey my thanks. I sent to ask him to send me a soldier who could train our men. He has sent me a Sergeant, an honest man, and I think, an able soldier who was in the German wars. Honest Petter is come out of prison. He was grievously used at Ludlow - Turks could not have used him worse. A lieutenant-colonel Marrow used to come every day and kick him up and down, and they laid him in a dungeon, on filthy straw. In Shrewsbury gaol he was better treated, but he is very glad to be home again.

June 30th: As you asked me to send you some honest men, I tried hard to find you some. Those that I thought would gladly have gone, found excuses, only three wished to venture their lives with you - otherwise they would not have left me. The poor gardener and Stangey volunteered themselves to go, and set off with good courage. I will see whether anyone will contribute towards buying a horse, but those that have hearts have no money, and those that have money have no hearts. I did not send Jack Griffiths because I thought you would prefer Philip Loukes, who is a clever fellow. If you would like to have Griffiths, let me know by Ralf and I will send him to you. Dear Ned, I could say more to you, but I have run out of paper.

LADY BRILLIANA DEFENDS HER CASTLE

July 11th, For my dear son, Colonel Harley: I am glad to let you know that I received your letter by Ralf. You can believe that it was very welcome, for I have long desired it. I thank the great mercy of my God that he saved your life in such a sharp battle, when your horse was killed. The Lord my God preserve you still. I am sorry that you lost so many of your troop but I hope that they will be made up again. I can get very little towards buying a horse, what I could get, I send you, enclosed. If you want anything I can possibly help you with, let me know it.

August 25th: I can only try to contact you, but I do not know you are in London or not. My dear Ned, the gentlemen of this county have had their way in raising an army against me. What damage has been done, this bearer will tell you. The Lord in his mercy preserve me, so that I do not fall into their hands. Mr. Philips has taken a great deal of trouble and is full of courage, as are all my household, with honest Mr. Petter and good Doctor Wright and Mr. Moore. This is a great comfort to me. May the Lord tell me what to do. Dear Ned, pray for me, that the Lord in His mercy will preserve me from my cruel and bloodthirsty enemies.

October 9th: Your short but welcome letter came by Prosser and I see that it has pleased God to entrust you with a greater command, changing your Troop into a Regiment. So may the Lord be your protector and make you victorious. If it pleased the Lord, I wish you were at Brampton, for I am again threatened. There are some soldiers come to Leominster and three troops of horse to Hereford, and they say they mean to visit Brampton again. I hope that the Lord will deliver me.

I have caught a great cold, which has made me very ill these last two or three days, but I hope the Lord will be merciful to me and give me good health, for it is a bad time to be ill. Dear Ned, I pray God bless you and give me the comfort of seeing you, for you are the comfort of your most affectionate mother,

Brilliana Harley.

A few days later, Lady Brilliana was dead. It was not her Royalist enemies, but her *great cold* which had killed her. Early in 1644 a fresh Royalist force attacked Brampton Castle. Dr. Wright and Sergeant Hackluit put up a brave defence, with only 70 men but the walls were broken down by cannon and the defenders captured with the three younger Harley children. The prisoners were sent to Shrewsbury gaol. Sir Robert's estate had lost £13,000 - and a gallant Lady.

LADY BRILLIANA'S CODE

Here is one of the letters which Lady Brilliana wrote to Ned in code. At first, it seems a meaningless jumble, but if you write out the words which are *in italics* you will find the hidden message. Of course, she did not make it as clear as that, there would be no difference in her handwriting. If you want to read the message as she sent it, this is what you do:

(1) Photocopy the letter from the book.

(2) Take a sheet of paper of **exactly** the same size and place it under the letter.

(3) Pierce holes with a pin, through both sheets of paper, marking the beginning and end of each word *in italics*.

(4) Remove the plain paper and draw lines between each pair of pin-holes, to mark the position of each word.

(5) With a razor-blade, carefully cut a window exactly one line deep, above each marked line.

(5) Now place the plain sheet over the photocopy. Read the message which shows in the windows. Brilliana would have sent the letter in one post and the cutout paper by a different messenger.

March 3rd, 1643.

My dear, *This day I* went above *hear that* great way so that they
pudd and *Sir William Croft* waters where first began *has sent forth*
I saw hard by *a warrant* too hard from the young men give and
Rich the that *to summon* same year for us and *24 men to come,*
they are forgotten and *into Herefordshire* and sister's children are
not, and are of opinion as those *on Monday* that are
next, to bear witness of a more constant mind and testament the
next in degree *to offences* can come to for they *and crimes* are
brother *laid to the* more kindred the greater affinity more a man is
charge of honoured is to be there *your father,* they must as well
become kinsmen yourself, or friends *yourself,* to their *Mr. James,*
friends satisfied, redeemed certain *and Mr. Gower* beasts common
with beasts and however *by Dickon* good for the liberty is there is
private of *the under* are not sensible I *sheriff* host will be to the
next. *The butler saw* for united will always be *the warrant* and are
received with courtesy and hospitality *in the bailiff's* of their
hand and make you no difference whether it be of or from or or a
he tore it up. Great, great will and *Meredith the* or not *ranger,* and
if anything the manor is to grant it demand or if so *Tom Child* you
and he *and Daley* as things ask the as things that please but those
that well being *of Leintwardine* do not *and Hopkins* thinker
of Downend that they you and bond or beholden them they enter
are some their geese *of the 24.* Which they wash warm having long
winter. *The rest of* and when seems *the names* they full *I know*
To eat every man stout *not.* I pray does not you send me
discourse or say nothing and the every means mind bring word
whether or is it to be it be so or the next or no, shall with or
regard. Your most affectionate Mother,

Brilliana Harley.

LADY BRILLIANA DEFENDS HER CASTLE

THE EVIDENCE

The Narrator: or letter-writer, **Lady Brilliana Harley (1600-43)**, was the third, much younger wife of **Sir Robert Harley (1579-1656)**. He was a leading Parliamentarian, after whose grandson, the second Earl of Oxford, the doctors' street in London is named. Brilliana was daughter of Sir Edward Conway of Rugby in the county of Warwick. Her father was a diplomat, Governor of the Brill in Holland, from which her name was taken. There she learned the strongly Puritan religious spirit which aroused the Roundhead opposition to King Charles and his bishops. Lady Fairfax, wife of the leading Roundhead general was a friend of Brilliana; she had also been brought up in Holland.

The collection of letters, found in the attic of a house by the Castle, survives both as originals and in print. They begin when her son Edward was a student at Magdalen College in Oxford and describe family life in Herefordshire at the outset of the Civil War. We learn a great deal of this lady's personality, her devout - and strict - religious faith, her generous nature and her great courage from her letters alone. The Harleys had seven children: Edward, Robert, Thomas, Brilliana, Dorothy, Margaret and Elizabeth.

A full account of Lady Brilliana's correspondence is given in *Herefordshire* by John and Margaret West (1985) and in the *Transactions of the Woolhope Naturalist & Field Club, Vol. 24 (1922)*. The complete collection of letters is printed in the 1854 volume of the *Camden Society,* edited by Thomas Taylor Lewis.

Documentary resources, pictures and contemporary texts, will be found in FACTPACK : *The English Civil War* (Ed: Douglas Clinton, ELM Publications 1989). This contains more than 60 original documents, including: contemporary maps of the campaigns, descriptions of the war by ordinary people, Generals' memoirs, statements of costs and payments for soldiers and armaments, pictures of uniforms, cannon and other weapons, and accounts of the trial and execution of Charles I.

CHECK THE EVIDENCE

Does Lady Brilliana seem to be a reliable witness and reporter? In what ways is she bound to be biased? Would this affect the accuracy of her reports?

In what way was she likely to have been well-informed about the war and the Parliamentary cause? Does this show at all in her letters? Is she well-informed? Lady Brilliana makes a great deal of religious comment. Is this likely to have influenced her writing?

Can you decode the letter on page 88 if it is re-typed *without italics*?

How can you set about checking the details of the Civil War in the western part of Britain? Does Lady Brilliana tell you anything that you might not be able to find in other books?

Make a list of any facts about the war, including famous names, places and events, which are mentioned in the letters. Check any history book about the Civil War and list any of its facts about the years 1642-3. Do your two lists match in any details?

What different sort of commentary might a *Royalist* lady have made on events in Herefordshire in 1643? In what different way might her religious views have been expressed? Do you think that the Cavaliers too, depended on God to help them win?

INFORMATION

After the first skirmish at Worcester, King Charles advanced towards London, which he had left in the hands of Parliament and their loyal Trained Bands. He was pursued by the Earl of Essex and his Roundheads. Prince Rupert persuaded the King to stand against the Parliamentary army at Edgehill, near Banbury (Oxfordshire). There the first major battle of the war was fought in October 1642, whilst Brampton was under siege. Each army totalled about 14,000 men.

After a reckless charge by Rupert, the Roundheads rallied and the Royal Standard was captured. Both sides claimed a victory. Although the way was now open to London, Charles was too cautious and let Essex get to the capital first. By the time the King reached the outskirts of the City, the London Trained Bands and Parliamentary soldiers barring his way numbered 24,000 men. The King withdrew to Oxford and never again entered London, except as a prisoner.

There were several battles, mostly Royalist victories, whilst Brilliana held on at Brampton. The siege began on 25th. July, 1643, during the same days that the port of Bristol was captured by Parliament. Sir William Vavassour brought up a force of 600 men, and surrounded the Castle for six weeks. The defenders were only 100 men, with two *drakes* or small cannon mounted on the walls and a bare two months supply of gunpowder. Parliament promised reinforcements but, apart from the veteran Sergeant Hackluit, all that came was an extra musket or two. During the attack, the Castle cook was killed by a poisoned bullet and the Royalists polluted Brampton's water supply. The church, mill, vicarage and surrounding houses were all destroyed, but the Castle held on. When called on to surrender, Lady Brilliana's answer was: "My Lord bids me hold!" On 22nd August, Vavassour was summoned to Gloucester by the King.

The Royalist siege of Gloucester in September 1643 was unsuccessful; Essex's relief column arrived just as the city's food and ammunition were exhausted. On 20th, at Newbury, trying to prevent Essex moving back to London, many Cavalier commanders were killed and Essex re-entered the city. He had reversed the tide of Royalist victories, but this did not help Lady Brilliana and her friends at Brampton. The survivors held out for nearly a year, but early in 1644, the year of the Parliament's resounding victory at Marston Moor, they surrendered. Only later still, after the most decisive Parliamentary victory of all, at Naseby in 1645, would the tide also turn in Herefordshire.

WHAT IS YOUR VERDICT?

One of the best and funniest of all History books, *1066 and all that!* by W.C. Sellar, R.J. Yeatman & John Reynolds (Methuen, 1984) describes the Victorian attitude to the Civil War exactly. For these authors, the Cavaliers were *Wrong but Romantic,* the Roundheads were *Right but Repulsive.* Was Lady Brilliana's character, as a Puritan, any more, or less Romantic than any Cavalier? Or, was she Repulsive in any way? Do you feel that her religious attitude was sincere?

The letters frequently say that she is not afraid. Do you detect any clues which reveal her fear? Did her husband and son treat her fairly? Was it right, or fair that Robert Harley left his wife alone, in charge of the Castle? Would he have been sexist to have felt that, as a woman, she was incapable of defending their home?

Was it selfish of Robert and Edward to write so infrequently? Did they have a genuine excuse? Notice how they ask her, hard-pressed as she was, to send *them* reinforcements.

Why should it surprise us that a woman of 1643 was able to take charge of her household and troops in a time of war? Do women have the same opportunities today?

Why do modern History books not tell us about other women like Brilliana? There is far more available evidence of Woman-History than has ever been written by sexist male historians. Find more examples of women in action for yourselves. Find out about WHAM! - the society which offers more information on Women in History and Museums (see Classroom Museum pages 295 - 296)

Notice how both parties used abusive terms to describe their enemies. In fact, both Cavalier - a bully, and Roundhead (an early version of skinhead), were originally unpleasant nicknames for the other side. To Lady Brilliana, all Royalists were malignants*, whilst the King's supporters described his enemies as rebels and traitors. Both sides were sure that they were in the right. What do you think? Which side would you have supported and why?

Who played the more useful part in the progress of the Civil War, Sir Robert or his wife? Debate this.

Do the Royalist officers and people around Lady Brilliana treat her any differently because she was a woman? Was their attitude more or less sexist than that of people like you, today?

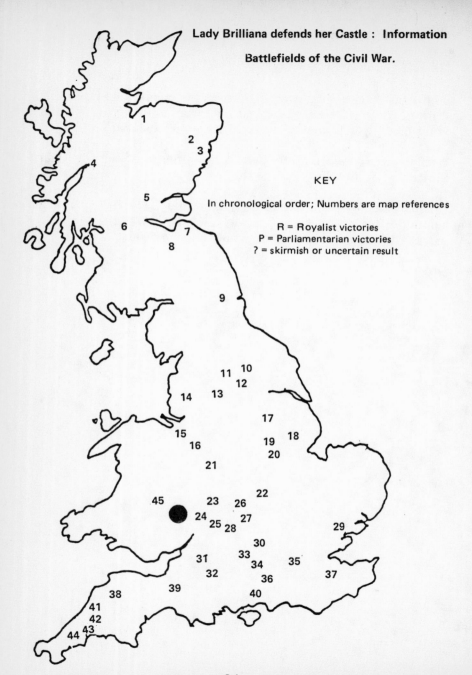

Lady Brilliana defends her Castle : Information

Battlefields of the Civil War.

KEY

In chronological order; Numbers are map references

R = Royalist victories
P = Parliamentarian victories
? = skirmish or uncertain result

The First Civil War 1640-1648

9	Newburn	(Northumberland)	August 1640	Scots
24	Powick Bridge	(Worcs)	September 1642	R
26	Edgehill	(Warwks)	October 1642	R?
35	Brentford	(London)	November 1642	R
43	Broad Oak Down	(Cornwall)	January 1643	R
25	Ripple Field	(Worcs)	March 1643	R
11	Seacroft Moor	(Yorkshire)	March 1643	R
12	Tadcaster	(Yorkshire)	March 1643	R
41	Stratton	(Cornwall)	April 1643	R
42	Launceston	(Cornwall)	April 1643	R
30	Chalgrove Field	(Oxon)	April 1643	R
21	Hopton Heath	(Staffs)	May 1643	R
20	Grantham	(Lincs)	May 1643	P
13	Adwalton Moor	(Yorkshire)	July 1643	R
31	Lansdown	(Somerset)	July 1643	R
32	Roundway Down	(Wiltshire)	July 1643	R
45	Brampton Bryan ●	(Herefs)	July 1643	R
17	Gainsborough	(Lincs)	August 1643	R?
33	Aldbourne Chase	(Wiltshire)	September 1643	?
38	Torrington	(Devon)	September 1643	R
34	Newbury (1)	(Berkshire)	September 1643	P
18	Winceby	(Lincs)	October 1643	P
36	Alton	(Hampshire)	December 1643	P
16	Nantwich	(Cheshire)	January 1644	P
40	Cheriton	(Hampshire)	March 1644	P
19	Newark	(Notts)	June 1644	R
27	Cropredy Bridge	(Oxon)	June 1644	R?
10	Marston Moor	(Yorks)	July 1644	P
5	Tippermuir	(Perthshire)	September 1644	R
44	Lostwithiel	(Cornwall)	September 1644	R
3	Aberdeen	(Aberdeenshire)	September 1644	R
34	Newbury (2)	(Berkshire)	October 1644	R?
4	Inverlochy	(Inverness-shire)	February 1645	R
1	Auldearn	(Nairnshire)	May 1645	R
2	Alford	(Aberdeenshire)	June 1645	R
22	Naseby	(Northants)	June 1645	P
39	Langport	(Somerset)	July 1645	P
6	Kilsyth	(Stirlingshire)	August 1645	R
8	Philiphaugh	(Selkirkshire)	September 1645	P
15	Rowton Heath	(Cheshire)	November 1645	P
42	Launceston	(Cornwall)	February 1646	P
28	Stow on the Wold	(Glos)	March 1646	P

● Scene of Lady Brilliana's siege.

The Second Civil War May 1648 to October 1651

37	Maidstone	(Kent)	June 1648	P
29	Colchester	(Essex)	July 1648	P
14	Preston	(Lancashire)	August 1648	P
7	Dunbar	(West Lothian)	September 1650	P
23	Worcester	(Worcs)	September 1651	P

THE BATTLE OF NASEBY

In 1645 the Civil War was at its height and the King's forces were losing ground. In June, Cromwell's New Model Army were chasing the Royalists from Daventry towards Leicester when Charles I decided to face them near Market Harborough. At first, Prince Rupert's cavalry drove off the Parliamentary horse but Cromwell's troopers stood firm and drove the Royalist infantry into confusion. The King's generals seized his horse's bridle and galloped from the scene, leaving 1,000 Cavaliers dead and 5,000 wounded. Two hundred years later, a famous historian and supporter of Parliament's cause wrote this poem in praise of the Roundhead victory.

It was about the noon of a glorious day in June,
　That we saw their banners dance, and their cuirasses* shine,
And the Man of Blood was there, with his long, scented hair,
　And Astley, and Sir Marmaduke and Rupert of the Rhine.

Like a servant of the Lord, with his Bible and his sword,
　The general rode along us to form us to the fight,
When a murmuring sound broke out, and swelled into a shout,
　Among the godless horsemen upon the tyrant's right.

And hark! like the roar of the billows on the shore,
　The cry of battle rises along their charging line!
For God! for the Cause! for the Church! for the Laws!
　For Charles King of England and Rupert of the Rhine!

The furious German comes, with his clarions and his drums,
　His bravoes* of Alsatia, and pages of Whitehall;
They are bursting on our flanks. Grasp your pikes, close your ranks;
　For Rupert never comes but to conquer or to fall.

THE BATTLE OF NASEBY

They are here! They rush on! We are broken! We are gone!
    Our left is borne before them like stubble on the blast.
O Lord, put forth thy might! O Lord, defend the right!
    Stand back to back, in God's name, and fight it to the last.

Stout Skipton hath a wound; the centre hath given ground:
    Hark! hark! - What means the trampling of horsemen on our
rear?
Whose banner do I see, boys? 'Tis he, thank God! 'tis he, boys,
    Bear up another minute: brave Oliver is here.

Their heads all stooping low, their points all in a row,
    Like a whirlwind on the trees, like a deluge on the dikes,
Our cuirassiers* have burst on the ranks of the accurst,
    And at a shock have scattered the forest of his pikes.

Fast, fast, the gallants ride, in some safe nook to hide
    Their coward heads, predestined to rot on Temple Bar:
And he - he turns, he flies: - shame on those cruel eyes
    That bore to look on torture, and dare not look on war.

Ho! comrades, scour the plain; and ere ye strip the slain,
    First give another stab to make your search secure,
Then shake from sleeves and pockets their broadpieces* and
lockets,
    The tokens of the wanton, the plunder of the poor.

Fools, your doublets shone with gold, and your hearts were gay
and bold,
    When you kissed your lily hands to your sweethearts today;
And tomorrow shall the fox, from her chambers in the rocks,
    Lead forth her tawny cubs to howl above the prey.

Where be your tongues that late mocked at heaven and hell and
fate,
   And the fingers that once were so busy with your blades,
Your perfumed satin clothes, your catches* and your oaths,
   Your stage-plays and your sonnets, your diamonds and your
spades?

Down, down, for ever down with the mitre* and the crown,
   With the Belial* of the Court, and the Mammon* of the Pope;
There is woe in Oxford Halls; there is wail in Durham's Stalls:
   The Jesuit smites his bosom; the Bishop rends his cope*.

And She of the seven hills* shall mourn her children's ills,
   And tremble when she thinks of the edge of England's sword;
And the Kings of earth in fear shall shudder when they hear
   What the hand of God hath wrought for the Houses and the
Word.

THE EVIDENCE

The Narrator: Thomas Babington, 1st Baron Macaulay (1800-59)
was son of a white West Indian merchant who campaigned for the
abolition of slavery. Macaulay was educated at private schools and
Trinity College, Cambridge, where he won prizes for English and
Latin verse. In 1824 he was elected Fellow of his College and
became a reluctant barrister in 1826. Preferring a literary career,
he contributed this poem and another on the Spanish Armada to
the *Knight's Quarterly Magazine* and wrote a famous article about
John Milton for the *Edinburgh Review*. In 1830 he was nomi-
nated for the pocket borough* of Calne in Wiltshire, but
supported the First Reform Bill of 1832, which abolished such
private Parliamentary constituencies.

From 1834-38 he worked as a legal adviser in Bengal, returning
home in 1839 to become MP for Edinburgh. He published his
famous *Lays of Ancient Rome* in 1842, but is most famous for his

KEY

denotes Cavalry units

denotes Foot soldiers

denotes Pike-men

1: Rupert's first charge
2: Cromwell's right-flanking move
3: Royalist Retreat

THE ROYALIST FORCES

The King's Majesty

K:
1: The King's Life Guards
2: Prince Rupert's Regiment of Foot
3: Prince Rupert's Horse
4: Colonel Howard
5: Sir Marmaduke Langdale
6: Sir Bernard Astley
7: Sir Henry Bard
8: Sir George Lisle
9: Sir Marmaduke Langdale and the Newark Horse

THE PARLIAMENTARY FORCES

The Left Wing commanded by General Ireton
The Right Wing commanded by Cromwell

I:
C:
9: Major General Skippon
10: Okey's Dragoons
11: Butler
12: Colonel Vermuyden
13-14: General Ireton's Regiment
15: Sir Hardress Waller
16: Colonel Pickering's Regiment
17: Montague's Regiment
18: Fairfax
19: Colonel Whalley
20: Sir Robert Pye
21: Colonel Rossiter

22: Rich
23: Colonel Fleetwood's Regiment
24: The Troops of the Association
25: Lieutenant Colonel Pride's Reserve
26: Colonel Hammond's Reserve
27: Colonel Rainborough's Reserve
28: Colonel Sheffield's Division
29: Sir Robert Pye
30: Colonel Fiennes
31: Rossiter
32: Lieutenant Colonel Pride's Rear Guard
33: The Association's Horse
34: Colonel Fiennes
35: Colonel Rossiter

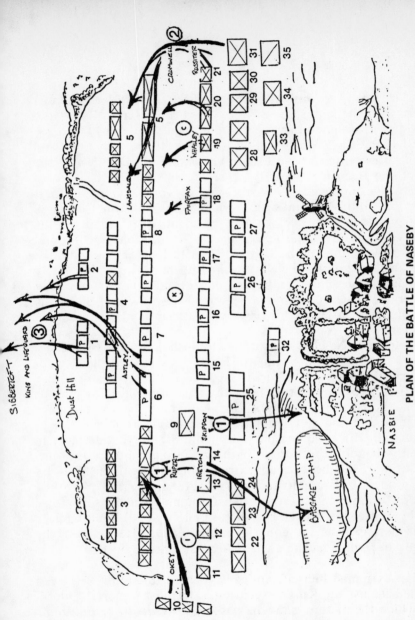

PLAN OF THE BATTLE OF NASEBY

HIS MAJESTIE'S ARMY of Horse and Foot, and of his Excellencies Sr.THOMAS FAIREFAX, as they were drawn into several Bodies.

BATTAIL OF NASBIE June the 14th. 1645 (As drawn by Josiah Sprigge)

classic *History of England,* (1848-1861). This deals almost entirely with the deposition of the Stuart King James II and the reigns of William and Mary. Thus, the reign of Charles I and the history of the Civil War is seen as a prelude to the inevitable and Glorious Revolution. The earlier history of England, from the time of the Romans is briefly sketched, in the first chapter of Volume One. Macaulay's History set up a model of history-writing for future generations, especially for Winston Churchill. Macaulay was responsible for the prevalent 19th century Whig myth, which glorified the Parliamentary Revolution of 1688 and took the perfection of the English constitution for granted. His impeccable style of writing was admired for many years, but lately there has been more criticism of several inaccuracies and considerable Whig bias in his work. He is also accused of letting personal dislike influence his views of politicians and events.

The Prospect of Naseby: was drawn by **Joshua Sprigg (1618-84)** a preacher who became a retainer of Fairfax, General of the Round-head New Model Army. He may have been an army chaplain, but it is difficult to say whether he actually accompanied the troops on their campaigns. Sprigg was born at Banbury; he was a student at Oxford, but did not graduate. Instead he took an MA at Edinburgh in 1639 and became preacher at St. Mary, Aldermary in London. He took the Puritan oath or Covenant before the outbreak of war and became an extreme Independent, disliked by more moderate Parliamentarian Presbyterians. He published books of sermons which even other Puritans called blasphemous, and when, after the war he became a Fellow of All Souls College he was described as far gone in enthusiasm*. He defaced the College gate, which had an ancient Ascension scene over it.

Being an extremist himself, Sprigg advocated toleration - he even preached against the King's execution. His most important work, from which the picture is taken, was *Anglia Rediviva* or *England's Recovery Being the History of the Motions, Actions and Successes* of the Army under his Excellency Sir Thomas Fairfax. This was published in 1647, based on pamphlets and newspapers of the period. It contains very little that was original, but was as accurate as his sources made it. Critics at the time referred to Sprigg's work as a legend or romance of the Army; some attributed it not to Sprigg, but to Nathaniel Fiennes, a more famous Parliamentarian on the spot.

CHECK THE EVIDENCE

Macaulay is a good example of a prejudiced historian. Check this poem and list the evidence of bias. What evidence is there, in the details of Macaulay's own political career, that he could behave impartially? How far is a writer's prejudice neutralised if we know what his viewpoint was, and what he is likely to say?

Man of Blood, tyrant and *Belial* of the Court.* These are Macaulay's terms of abuse for the King. His followers are godless horsemen, the ranks of the accurst, who hide their coward heads. They mocked heaven and bore to look on torture. Can you find evidence to prove these descriptions to be true?

See how some special words, like *bravoes* and *gallants,* even *sweethearts,* become specially vicious nicknames - like Cavalier and Roundhead. Is Macaulay's 19th century Puritan language any easier to understand than Lady Brilliana's genuine 17th century words? Compare Macaulay's view of Cavaliers with the painter Yeames. Is there a similar Victorian attitude in both?

Notice the deeply religious antagonism of the poem, especially to Rome and the Pope. Compare Lady Brilliana's religious attitude and decide if her views are similar to Macaulay's. Does the poem describe the Civil War as a religious dispute or a political rebellion?

Of course, Macaulay might answer criticism of his own prejudice by saying that he was correctly portraying what any convinced Roundhead would have thought and said. What do you think?

THE BATTLE OF NASEBY

Notice, strangely how Macaulay seems to glory in the idea of the victorious New Model soldiers stabbing and robbing wounded Royalists. How does this make you feel about Roundheads? Did Macaulay intend this?

After all, it is a stirring poem, with a lively rhythm and a bold attack on the story. Does this make reliable History too? Does it matter that Macaulay is writing 200 years after the battle? What were his sources likely to have been?

Does Joshua Sprigg's picture of the battle match our diagram?

INFORMATION

In July 1644, at Marston Moor the Royalist army lost 4,000 men and ceased to exist as an organised force. Meanwhile, a turncoat Covenanter, the Marquis of Montrose, became commander of the King's army in Scotland, where he won a series of Royalist victories. As the war dragged on, his native Scots became the Stuart king's last hope. In the summer of 1645, Charles marched northward to join Montrose. His followers urged him to turn back to defend his base at Oxford, which was under attack. The two armies met on 14th. June at Naseby, near Market Harborough in Leicestershire. The Roundheads took up their position on a ridge in front of Naseby, with low marshy ground to their front. The Royalists moved across the low ground, but Ireton drove back Rupert's cavalry. A second charge broke Ireton's line and Rupert, though he was the King's Commander-in-Chief, made his usual mistake and chased the Roundhead cavalry back to their baggage camp. Cromwell attacked on the right flank, creating confusion. By the time that Rupert rode back to the field, the battle was lost and Fairfax occupied the original Royalist position as the Cavaliers fled.

Naseby was the decisive defeat of Charles's army. His infantry was totally destroyed and 500 officers captured, with the Royal artillery and baggage. The Roundheads savagely massacred the Cavaliers' camp-followers, branding many prostitutes with hot irons. The Civil War was virtually over, though Charles continued to seek support. In September 1645, as Royalist strongholds in the west were mopped up by Fairfax, a disbelieving King heard news of Montrose's decisive defeat at Piliphaugh. Montrose fled to Norway, but returned, proclaiming his loyalty to Charles Stuart and was hanged by the Covenanters in 1650. In March 1646 the King attempted a secret treaty with the Scots and, disguised as a servant, wandered off from Oxford to attempt an escape by sea. A Scottish escort, sent to meet him, took the King prisoner instead. In June 1646, Prince Rupert surrendered Oxford. This is referred to as the end of the First Civil War. With Charles I a prisoner, all future Royalist resistance was left to his son, Charles, first as Prince of Wales, then as Charles II.

WHAT IS YOUR VERDICT?

The battles and causes of the Civil War seem so far off that it is difficult for us to understand their violent passions in modern terms. Were the loyalties and passions of both sides more real or more righteous than those behind modern warfare? Do the small-scale, but violent struggles in Lebanon, the Philippines, Rumania, and Ethiopia bear any resemblance to earlier civil war?

If the whole political and religious conflict has become meaningless to us, does it become just a sort of adventure yarn? Or should we look for deeper motives and beliefs which were worth dying for? Does the Royalist cause arouse more sympathy in us as a lost cause? Is this a sensible view of real events?

ESCAPE FROM CARISBROOKE?

For a few months after his almost final defeat at Naseby, Charles I wandered about England, whilst his surviving generals raised Royalist uprisings in the north and west. The King turned secretly from one possible ally to another. In April 1646 he left Oxford in disguise and headed for the coast. Arrested by enemy soldiers, he was kept prisoner in various castles. Still he tried to outwit his captors. This story of the King's attempt to escape, was told to me, as it has been told to children, by Dr. John Fines, as follows:-

It is 1648. King Charles I is imprisoned in Carisbrooke Castle on the Isle of Wight. His enemies are divided into three groups - Parliament, the Scots and the Army. As soon as they can come together, they will kill him. Fortunately for the King, they cannot agree and he tries to deal with each of his enemies in turn. This makes them distrust him all the more. He lives in one small bedroom, with two doors, both with guards, and a barred window. At night the guards push their beds against the door.

When Henry Firebrace arrived at the Castle, everyone thought he was a Parliament man. He had been Secretary to the Earl of Denbigh for the past few months and the Earl was a very strong Parliament man, who had fought against the King at Edgehill. So the guards trusted him and King Charles, in public, treated him as an enemy. But the King had known Firebrace before, as a servant at Court, and he began to wonder whether Henry might not be a friend after all. The only ally he really had at that time, was Mary, the laundry maid, who slipped letters underneath the carpet in his room and collected the King's secret letters from the same place, to send on to his followers. Perhaps it was Mary who told the King that Firebrace was a true friend?

One night, Henry persuaded one of the guards that he would do his duty for him, and whispered to the King through a small barred window. He had a plan for an escape. The King should get out of the window, climb down a rope, and Firebrace would get him over the two walls of the Castle, where horsemen would be ready to take him to a boat to escape overseas. Firebrace urged to King to see if he could get out of the window. The King said that he had tried putting his head through and that was easy. Henry asked him to try to push his shoulders through, but the King grew impatient and angry at being told what to do by one of his subjects. Henry was afraid that people would hear his raised voice.

On the night they had agreed. Firebrace was standing beneath the window, and heard the King start to get out. After a little while, he heard a terrible groan, then nothing more for a while. Then he saw a lighted candle in the window, which was their signal to call off the operation. He threw some gravel over the Castle wall, to warn his friends, and heard the jingle of the horses' harness as they moved away. The escape had failed.

Then Firebrace persuaded Charles to try to take out one of the window-bars. The King began patiently filing one of the bars, but soon lost patience and gave up any further attempts to escape. Firebrace stayed with the King until they took him away from the island, to try him and execute him. When they were taking the King away, Firebrace made some breakfast for him, but it took so long to get the fire going that the King could not eat a bit of it and was hustled into his coach. Firebrace remembered that the Deputy Governor tried to get into the coach with the King, as a guard, but the King indignantly pushed him out of the coach, saying, "It hasn't come to that yet."

On the day before his execution, Charles I remembered Firebrace and told his chaplain* to make sure that his son, the Prince of Wales, would look after the man "who has been very faithful and serviceable to me in my great difficulties". Henry went back to being Secretary to the Earl of Denbigh but when Charles I's son came to the throne in 1660, Henry asked the new King for one of his earlier royal positions. Charles II made him, not only Chief Clerk of the Kitchen, but also Clerk Controller of the Household and Assistant to the Officers of the Royal Household. Henry also received a pension of £1,694 - a very large sum of money in those days. He lived on until he was 72 years of age. His second wife was an unknown woman named Mary.

THE EVIDENCE

The Narrator: **Dr. Fines** was not the original Narrator, only the Story-teller. He is a modern historian, Fellow of the Royal Historical Society and Vice President of the Historical Association. He specialises in studies of the early 16th century and we have already used his material on *The Pilgrimage of Grace.* John Fines is a teacher who works with children in all parts of the country. He is often asked to create stories that fit places. When he was asked to visit Carisbrooke Castle, he obviously wanted to find the most important event in its history, in order to tell its story.

Henry Firebrace (1619-91) surely must have told his story many times in his old age. He was the sixth son of Robert Firebrace of Derby and entered the royal household service as page of the Bedchamber. He became Yeoman of the Robes and Clerk of the Kitchen to Charles I, positions which he gained by favour of the Earl of Denbigh. He had helped the King before, at Oxford in 1644 and after Charles's surrender to the Scots was with him at Newcastle, Holmby House and Hampton Court. His position at Carisbrooke, as a man of 29, was that of Page to the Bedchamber. He is buried in Westminster Abbey.

The Story: The original sources of this story were 17th century pamphlets, news-sheets and letters. Using these, Jack Jones wrote *The Royal Prisoner,* published by the Trustees of Carisbrooke Castle in 1965. This was Dr. Fines's main source for his story-telling.

ESCAPE FROM CARISBROOKE?

CHECK THE EVIDENCE

How many times removed from the original event of nearly 350 years ago is Dr. Fines's story? If you wanted to check whether he had told the story accurately, where would you look for any other evidence?

What would Firebrace's motives have been in making sure that his help to the King became well known later? Would this have affected the facts he included? After all, the escape never took place, no-one could have been told at the time, only much later when memories were failing. Could Henry have made the whole thing up for a reward?

Collect other romantic tales of the adventures and escapes of Charles I and his son, Charles II. Does the history of a series of events become unreliable if it is made too romantic? Or, is it just that some events are full of clever plots and colourful characters?

INFORMATION

Charles I (1625-49): was born in 1600 (the same year as Lady Brilliana Harley) and was second son of King James I, the first Stuart King of England. His elder brother Henry died, so Charles - his father always referred to him as Baby Charles - became King in 1625. His high-handed policies, disregard of Parliament's opposition, innovative taxes, and above all, his High Church, suspected Catholic religion, brought the country to Civil War in 1642.

The King's habitual indecision, poor man-management and lack of capable advisers, as well as the ruthless efficiency of his enemies, caused his defeat and execution. His reign, it was said: "both in peace and war, was a continual series of errors..." The King's own sad final judgment was "There was never a man so alone as I .... " "Men wondered", wrote one Puritan lady, "that so good a man could be so bad a king." His love for his wife and children was touching, and he met his death with dignity and courage, wearing an extra shirt on that cold January day, so that none might think that he trembled with fear. To his Judges - whom he absolutely refused to acknowledge - he had been a tyrant, a traitor, a murderer and public enemy. He was a victim of the traditional but outworn Divine Right of Kings.

WHAT IS YOUR VERDICT?

Children who have been told this story discussed a number of questions about the King's behaviour and about Henry Firebrace. Some of these were: Why did the King not check whether he could get through the window? What do you think the groan meant? Children at Carisbrooke found 12 different explanations for this. How many can you find?

Why did Firebrace serve the Parliamentarian Earl of Denbigh (twice) if he was really a Royalist? On the other hand, how could he return to the service of Charles II if he was really a Roundhead?

Do you think that Firebrace was properly rewarded for what he did? Clerk of the Kitchen was one of the many jobs that had a salary from the King, but other, humbler people did the dirty work. The word for this type of job is a *sinecure*. Are there any similar posts today? For example, the Chairman of British Rail earns a great deal of money without ever driving a railway engine! Firebrace's appointments, like all ancient royal positions, have wonderfully high-sounding names. Perhaps you can invent some for yourself and your friends?

In telling me this story, Dr. Fines omitted to mention that Firebrace had previously been in the royal employment, before the war; that Charles I remembered him and recommended him to his son; that Charles II gave him more than one royal appointment; that Firebrace also received a large pension, and that he is buried in Westminster Abbey. Was he quite fair to Charles I?

Charles I was evidently a difficult man to help. Why was this? What aspects of his character made him refuse to co-operate enough for Firebrace's plans to work? Work out your own estimation of the King's character and behaviour, based upon as many different aspects of the evidence as possible. Begin two lists, For and Against the King.

Perhaps the most romantic mystery of all is the identity of Henry's unknown second wife, named Mary. Could she possibly have been .... ?

'AND WHEN DID YOU LAST SEE YOUR FATHER?'

On January 31st. 1649, King Charles I was executed after after a trial which he refused to answer. In February, Parliament abolished Kingship in England, but Charles I's 19-year-old son was already acclaimed by Royalists as Charles II. The young king faced his enemies near Worcester, but was soundly defeated by Cromwell. He escaped from the battlefield and wandered first northward, then southward, towards the coast. For six weeks, in disguise, he escaped from his pursuers. His loyal followers hid him in their houses, in cheese-lofts, cellars and priests' holes, even, once in an oak-tree.

After any great defeat like Worcester, wounded Cavaliers also made secretly for home, riding by night to avoid triumphant Roundhead patrols. Their families, like Lady Brilliana on the other side, waited anxiously for their menfolk's safe return. Without newspapers, radio, TV or telephones, news travelled slowly. Parliament's officials sometimes came first, to cross-question wives and children about their Cavalier's whereabouts. Sometimes, they hoped, they might find a wounded fugitive hiding in the manor-house, protected by his family.

Nearly 250 years after those troubled times, a Victorian artist painted the dramatic scene which we see in our picture. He imagined what it must have been like, to be a Royalist family facing interrogation by Parliament's men. He shows a small boy being questioned by investigators, who hope that the child will innocently give his father away. They have treated him kindly, but at last they try to trap him with the dangerous question: "And when did you last see your father?" We too, can try to describe, in words, this dramatic moment, as the painter saw it. We can only imagine the thoughts of the little boy as he stands, silent on the stool before the table. He does not speak a word.

"Stand here my child and speak to us."

(*He thinks:*) "This fellow speaks to me as if I were a babe. I am not a child. I am eight years old. My father said that, whilst he is away, I must be the man of the house. I serve our Mother as he serves the King. I will stand tall and teach them manners."

"Stand on that stool boy, that we may see you better."

"I am very frightened. Little sister Pen is frightened too, for she has begun to cry. Does this fellow mean to be kind to me? His voice is soft, and he speaks kindly, but he is Cromwell's man. All these are Parliament rogues. Father says that all the rotten Rump* are against God and King. Their troopers treated the old vicar cruelly and stabled their horses in our chapel. No Christian would behave so!"

"Now, there are many matters that you can help us with, Hugh. I am told that you are a helpful boy, and truthful too."

"Say nothing, Hugh", big sister Lucy told me. She was very cross with me. "You prattle, Hugh," she said, "and tattle to the servants." That is not true. I spoke only with Jem Stables about the strange horses I saw in the paddock. I do not tell tales and I will not speak, even though they may beat me. Anyway, Jem already knew about those horses."

"You understand that you must help us. We are sent to keep the peace."

"Lucy says that this is the rebels' Commissioner for our county. She said that Parliament have tried the King and done him to death like a common criminal. This surely cannot be true? No man's court can try a King and Mother still prays for King Charles. Father too, as he rode away, said that he would join the King at Worcester. I know that Lucy is keeping a secret. Does Mother know it too? I am almost sure she does, but she said, very clearly, that Father is not at home now, and Mother never lies. So I must be mistaken."

"Come now lad, be not afraid to speak to us."

"The trooper is kind enough, even though he is a Roundhead. He is Jem Stables' brother-in-law. Jem does not speak to him any more, since he joined the rebels' army, nor to his own sister either."

"I'll make the young malignant* speak, Brother Amos!"

"That other one is not kind at all. Nor are his manners any better. He sits there, sprawled with his legs a-straddle, as if this were a tavern. He was my Father's tenant before Parliament seized our lands as a punishment. As long as he demands, I will not speak."

"It will save your soul to speak the truth to us, young fellow. Remember that God is your witness."

"This fellow now, with the tall hat and the long nose, has no manners either. None of these ranting* Puritans has the courtesy to uncover, even in a lady's presence. They say they honour no man, only God himself. This creature is Master Hopkins, who fancies himself as our village preacher since the old Vicar was sent away. Praise-God Hopkins he calls himself now, though his baptismal name was Ebenezer. When my uncle George was Sheriff, this pretender was arrested for writing evil little books against my Lord the Bishop. 'Twas a pity they did not crop his ears for him, as well as keeping him in the pillory* for three days and nights. I will not answer him. The kind one does not wish me to anyway. He shrugs the ranter off impatiently."

"Pay attention lad! Your mother has said that your father was wounded at Worcester field a fortnight since. What do you know of that?"

"Don't answer! They know that Father rode with the King's troop, why does he ask me that? He cannot know what I saw last

— 115 —

night. But what he asks about was not last night. It was near a week ago that George Vernon and Jem brought father's horse home, riderless. There was noise in the stable yard and I woke to hear Steward John call for grooms and darkened lights. My room is above the court and hooves on the cobbles always waken me. I woke gladly, being sure that Father and Ralf had returned from Worcester. Lucy believes that Father is dead. George Vernon gave her Father's sash, his sword and purse, she said. She does not know that I saw them too, from my window by moonlight. There was blood on the sash. Is my Father dead? Mother told them that he was wounded and taken to his bed at Lady Vernon's house in the south county. Perhaps Lucy is wrong and he isn't dead?"

"Speak up, you young scoundrel. You keep us waiting!"

"Now the other fellow at the table, with the surly face. He was my Uncle Harry's land-agent last year. He calls himself Leveller Jenkins now, and commanded the traitor Birch's pikes when Goodrich Castle was taken. This upstart spoke roughly to my Mother just now. The Commissioner asked her pardon. Lucy will never cry. Tell them nothing, Hugh, she said. Not even your name. Lucy would lie, to save my father, whatever Mother says."

"You were all together here this Summer, were you not? I expect you played in all the hiding-holes about this house?"

"He'll not get that from me! Father is not in the old priest-hole. I hid there yesterday, from Pen. She thinks that she knows all the secret places, but she never found old Father Oldham's nook under the fifteenth stair. They lit the fires this afternoon. "To smoke cavalier vermin out of the chimney-piece and wainscote*", the rough fellow said. They know about the secret panel in the Hall. Father always hid his letter-box behind it, and the bearded one is holding that. They have Father's secret letters on the table before them. I can recognize Grandfather's green seal on some of them. Shall I tell them something we know they have already?

Then perhaps they will leave me be? No, Lucy said: "Say nothing Hugh." I will not answer that."

"Your father has always taught you to tell the truth, has he not?"

"There was noise in the stable yard again last night. The riders had muffled their horses' hooves and bound the harness, but couldn't keep the horses quiet. I was sure that this must be Father and Ralf, home at last. I couldn't see clearly, though there was a moon. The rider was taller than my Father, and might have been very swarthy*, though the light was bad and darkened skin is a good disguise at night. His companion was dismounted, helping him down. Our servants knelt there, on the cobbles. They never kneel for Father, he would find that very strange. Lucy made courtesy too, but surely she would have embraced the man, had it been our Father? Mother stayed in the house, calling for Steward John and the house-servants, as if to receive an honoured guest. The other man led off the horses secretly, without a groom to help him. But he didn't stable them, they were hidden in the far paddock this morning. They were not my Father's greys, but country hacks, blown and hard-ridden. Perhaps the servants knelt because Father was lately with the King? Lucy told them none of this, nor Mother either. I will not answer."

"Come now, there must be something you can say to help us. You wouldn't wish to make me angry, would you? What guests have slept here lately?"

"I will not answer. I cannot answer, because I truly do not know. Perhaps it wasn't Father after all? I ran downstairs, but it was so dark in the courtyard and I was frightened. When Jem Stables caught me hiding behind the outhouse door, he held his big smelly hand over my mouth to stop me crying out. "God be praised," Jem muttered, as if I wasn't there. "They've brought him safe from Worcester field." So is Father within the house or safe in Lady Vernon's Hall, as Mother told them? Father would have sent for me, to greet me, if he were here."

"They helped the big man down and almost carried him into the house. He laid his hand on Sister Lucy's bowed head, almost as a bishop or courtly nobleman would bless her. I wonder where they hid him? He must be under the floor of the cheese-loft if he's not in the priest-hole. Mother was very pale when she led them there. They took their dogs with them, but they'd sniff out nothing more than cheese. Mother told this fellow that she had not seen Father since he rode away last month. And Mother never lies. I wish so much that they had told me what it is I mustn't say. I wish my father were here to help me. It troubles me to fear that I may never see him again. Is he in this house, even now?"

"And when did you last see your father .... ?"

THE EVIDENCE

The Painter: William Frederick Yeames RA (1835-1918) was born in Russia, where his father was British Consul. He lived in Odessa and Dresden, returned to England and studied in London, then in Florence and Rome. He lived in Italy from 1852-8, exhibited at the Royal Academy and retired in 1913. He specialised in scenes from English History, especially from Elizabethan times and the Civil War. Yeames is typical of the Victorian 'narrative' painters and this is his most famous painting.

The Author: John West (1926-) was a History teacher who has written several books for teachers and children. He has read about the Civil War in History books and studied some original documents about the subject, both in print and as originals. This is not however, really his period. He lives within the area of King Charles II's flight from Worcester and has visited several of the houses, like Boscobel and Moseley Old Hall, where the King hid.

CHECK THE EVIDENCE

Compared with the original evidence of other stories in this book, you may feel that both picture and story are fakes. The picture is not the record of any event which really happened, nor of any known family. We can only say that such an incident *might have* happened. Yeames explained his painting: "I had, at the time I painted the picture, living in my house, a nephew of an innocent and truthful disposition, and it occurred to me to represent him in a situation where the child's outspokenness and unconsciousness would lead to disastrous consequences. A scene in a country house, occupied by the Puritans during the Rebellion in England, suited my purpose." We do not know what other sources Yeames may have used to make his picture accurate. Check details of costume and furniture in reference books.

The author was inspired by the painting to imagine what the boy's feelings might have been. So, painting and story, each takes one more step away from real History. Does this mean that we can learn nothing useful from either painting or story? What facts can you check in each? Can you tell whether either the painter or the author is more sympathetic to Royalists or Roundheads? The painter gives himself away in something he wrote. Perhaps there are other clues?

INFORMATION

Victorian Narrative Painters (See page 76): The Civil War was the most popular Victorian subject. Paintings include: *A wounded Cavalier* (William Shakespeare Bruton, 1856); *The proscribed* Royalist* (William Henry Simmons, 1853); *The mocking of Charles I, and Cromwell gazing at the body of Charles I* (Paul Delaroche, 1831 and 1837) and *The parting of Charles I with his two youngest children on the day before his execution* (Charles Lucy, 1852). These, and many more, are illustrated in by Roy Strong in his book, also called *'And when did you last see your father?'* (Thames & Hudson, 1978) See also: Christopher Wood's *Dictionary of Victorian Painters* (Antique Collectors' Club, 1978).

'AND WHEN DID YOU LAST SEE YOUR FATHER?'

Many Victorian writers describe the Civil War in a disapproving way, as a Rebellion against a tragic King, who goes nobly to his death. Like old cowboy films, there is no doubt about the Good guys and the Bad guys. Victorian History is full of Good Kings and Bad Kings, simple heroes and dramatic villains. Critics condemn their story-pictures as sentimental, Jingoistic or just poor History. Yeamses's picture tells more about Victorian ideas than real Royalist and Roundhead attitudes. Lately there have been several Exhibitions of these paintings, which are now seen to be an interesting source of Victorian History.

You might prefer to see contemporary, seventeenth century story-pictures about the Civil War. If you look at some of the 17th century landscapes or portraits in Art Galleries however, you will see that they are very different from Victorian narrative paintings - certainly not as dramatic! For a set of contemporary documents, notes and pictures of the Civil War see FACTPACK No:6 *Cromwell* (Ed: Douglas Clinton, ELM Publications, 1988). This contains the most dramatic picture of all, that of Cromwell's death-mask in gruesome colour. There are also portraits, pictures of artefacts, facsimile documents and original prints, such as Sprigg's view of the Battle of Naseby.

WHAT IS YOUR VERDICT?

Do you remember 1066 and all that? Which of the characters in Yeames's painting were right or wrong, and which were more romantic or repulsive. Did either the painter or the author of the story get it right, or are both too sentimental? Whose side would you have taken?

A critic wrote that "By 1878, the theme of Cavaliers and Round-heads had been reduced to what seems to us little more than an episode from a children's adventure story." Is there anything very wrong in this - for children? Is our story any different? Is imagination of any use in learning History? Why not try to write your own History stories, or paint their pictures.

BRING OUT YOUR DEAD!

> Towns were growing up all over England during the Tudor and Stuart period. They were dangerous, insanitary places, over-crowded and undrained. The great plague described in this story, written day by day by a man who lived through it, was only one of many epidemics during the seventeenth century. The account was written by Samuel Pepys, a busy civil servant at the Navy Office in London. His story is told by extracts from a private diary which he kept throughout the days of the plague, beginning with the first rumours of sickness, heard around the City in April 1665.

1665: Sunday, 30th. April: I end this month in great content as to my estate and profits. There are great fears of the sickness here in the City, it being said that two or three houses are already shut up. God preserve us all!"

June 7th: This day, much against my will, I did in Drury Lane see two or three houses marked with a red cross upon the doors and *LORD HAVE MERCY UPON US* written there. This was a sad sight to me, being the first of that kind that I can remember ever having seen. It put me into an unpleasant mood with myself and my smell, so that I was forced to buy some roll tobacco to smell and to chew, which took away my fears.

June 11th: Up and expected the delivery of a new suit, but, when it did not come I dresses myself in my last black silk camelot* suit. Then, when I was fully dressed, comes my new one of coloured ferrandin* which my wife puts me out of love with, which vexes me. I think that it is only my not being used to wearing colours, which look a little unusual on me. I went out of doors a while, to show my new suit forsooth, then back indoors again. In doing so, I saw poor Dr. Burnett's door shut. He hath, I hear, gained great goodwill amongst his neighbours, because, recognizing the symptoms himself, he caused himself to be shut up

SAMUEL PEPYS

of his own accord. Which was very handsome. In the evening came Mr. Andrews and his wife, and Mr. Hill. They stayed and played and sang and supped - most excellent, pretty company!

June 16th: Up and to the office, where I set hard to business. I was informed that the Duke of York has come and has made an appointment for us to attend on him this afternoon. So, after dinner, I went to Whitehall, where the Court was full of the Duke and his courtiers, returned from sea, all fat and lusty and ruddy from the sun. It struck me very deeply this afternoon, going with a hackney-coach* from my Lord Treasurer's down Holborne when I found the coachman driving more and more slowly. At last he stopped and got down, hardly able to stand. He told me that he was suddenly struck very sick and almost blind. So I got out and went on in another coach, with a sad heart for the poor man, and for myself also, lest he might have been struck by the plague, it being at the end of the town that I took him up. God have mercy on us all! Sir Joseph Lawson, I hear, is worse than yesterday. His wound is not very bad, but he hath a fever and a thrush* and a Hiccup, all three together, which are, it seems, very bad symptoms.

June 20th: Thanksgiving Day for victory over the Dutch. Up and to the office, where I was very busy, all alone all the morning until church-time. To the *Dolphin Tavern,* where all we Officers of the Navy met with the Commissioners of Ordnance by agreement and dined. We had some good music, at my direction. Our club came to 34 shillings a man and there were nine of us. Went by water to Foxhall* and there walked for an hour alone, watching the various pleasures of the citizens who were out there this holiday, picking cherries and God knows what. Today I found out that four or five people died at Westminster of the plague on Sunday last, that is in Bell Alley over by the Palace gates. Some people think that the number will be fewer in town than last week.

June 29th: Up and by water to Whitehall, where the Court is full of waggons with people ready to leave town. This end of town grows very bad of the plague, every day. The Mortality Bill* is come to 267, which is about 90 more than last week's. Of these, there were only 4 in the City, which is a great relief to us. Home, calling at Somerset House, where they were all packing up. The Queen Mother is setting out for France today to drink the Bourbon waters - she is suffering from consumption - and does not intend to come back until winter twelve months on.

July 29th: (Lord's Day) Up and in my nightgown*, nightcap and neck-cloth, stayed undressed all day long. I lost not a minute, but worked in my Chamber, setting my Tangier accounts to rights. Will was with me today and is very well again. It was a sad noise to hear our church bell toll so often today, either for deaths or burials, I think five or six times. By nightfall I was weary with the day's work, but joyful at having done it. Only under some difficulty because of the plague, which grows strongly upon us, the last week being about 1,700 or 1,800. My Lord Sandwich is at sea with a fleet of about 100 ships, sailing northward and expecting the Dutch East India Fleet.

August 8th: Up and to the office, where we sat all the morning. At noon, home to dinner alone. The streets are empty all the way now, even in London, which is a sad sight. Then to Westminster Hall, where, talking to people, I hear many sad stories. Among others, of poor Will, who used to sell us ale at the Hall door - his wife and three children died, all in one day. So home, throughout the City again, hoping that I have taken no ill in going there.

August 10th: My cousin Porter tells me that her husband was taken to the Tower for buying some of the King's gunpowder, and wanted my help. I can give her none, not daring to appear in the investigation. By and by to the office where we sat all morning. In great trouble to see this week's Bill rise so high, more than 4,000 in all, and of these, more than 3,000 of plague. Home, to draw up my will again, the town growing so unhealthy that a man cannot depend on living for two days.

August 12th: People die so rapidly that now, it seems, they must carry out the dead to be buried in daylight, the nights are not long enough. My Lord Mayor orders everyone to be indoors by 9 at night, so that the sick shall be free to go out for fresh air. There is also a man dead on one of our ships at Deptford, which troubles us very much - the *Providence* fireship, just fitted out to go to sea. But, they tell me today, there are no more sick men on board. I am also told that the wife of one of the grooms at Court is dead at Salisbury, so that the King and Queen have gone very quickly off to Wilton. So God preserve us all! It was dark before I could get home, so I landed at Churchyard steps. Where, to my great horror, I met a corpse, dead of the plague, being carried down the narrow alley, and down the little steps. But I thank God, I was not much disturbed by it. However, I shall beware of being out late again.

August 16th: To the Exchange again, where I have not been for a great while. But, Lord! what a sad sight it is, to see the streets empty of people, afraid of every door one sees shut up, in case it is the plague. About 2 in every 3 shops, if not more, are shut up. This day I had the bad news that my poor Lord of Hinchinbrook's illness has turned into smallpox. Poor gentleman! Our fleet is home, to our great grief, with no more than five weeks' dry and six days' wet provisions. However, it must sail out again. This news troubles us, but it cannot be helped. So to sleep, being very well, but weary and the better for having carried a bottle of strong water, whereof, now and then, a sip did me good.

August 31st: Thus this month ends, with great sadness on the public through the great extent of the plague, everywhere throughout the kingdom. Almost every day, there is sadder and sadder news of its increase. In the City this week 7,496 died, 6,102 of plague. But they fear that the true number is nearer 10,000, partly because of the poor people, who cannot be taken notice of because they are so many, and partly because of the Quakers and others who will not have any bell rung for them.

September 3rd: Up and put on my coloured silk suit, very fine, and my new periwig*, bought a long while ago, but I dare not wear it, because the plague was in Westminster when I bought it. It is to be wondered what the fashion in periwigs will be, after the plague is done, for no-one will dare buy any hair for fear of infection - in case it was cut off the heads of people dead of the plague. Among other stories, one was very sad, I thought, of a complaint against a man for taking a child out of an infected house. He had buried all the rest of his children of the plague. He and his wife, now being shut up, and in despair of escaping, desired only to save the life of this little child. So, he arranged to have it received, stark naked, into the arms of a friend, who brought it, (having put it into new, fresh clothes), to Greenwich. Where, upon hearing the story, we agreed that it should be permitted to be received and kept in the town.

September 5th: After dinner Colonel Blunt came in his new carriage, made with springs. It outdrives any coach and outgoes any horse, and so comfortable, (so he says). So, for curiosity, I went into it, to try it, and drove up Shooters Hill to Blackheath and over the cart-ruts and found it pretty good - but not as comfortable as he pretends.

September 15th: Though the Bill in general is smaller, yet in the City, within the walls, it has increased, and likely to continue so - and it is close to our house there. Meeting corpses, dead of the plague, being carried to be buried close to us at noonday, through the City - to see a person sick with the sores, being carried close by me in a hackney-coach - finding the Angel Tavern at the lower end of Tower Hill shut up, as well as the Alehouse at Tower Stairs - to hear that poor Payne, my waterman has buried a child and is dying himself - and that one of my watermen*, who carried me daily, fell sick as soon as he had landed me last Friday morning, and is now dead - to hear that Captains Lambert and Cuttle are dead on taking over their ships and that Mr. Sidney Montague is sick of a desperate fever - to hear that Mr. Lewis has another daughter sick and lastly, that both my servants, Will Ewers and Toma Edwards, have lost their fathers of plague this week - all this puts me into great fears and sadness, with good reason. But I put off all thoughts of sadness as much as I can, to keep my wife and family in good heart.

September 18th: By break of day we came in sight of the Fleet, which was a very fine thing to behold, being more than 100 ships, both great and small, with the flagships of each squadron identified by their different flags on their fore, main or mizzen* masts. We came on board the Prince and found my Lord Sandwich nearly up, in his nightgown, very well. He received us kindly, telling us the state of the fleet, lacking provisions, having no beer at all, nor have had, most of them, these three weeks or a month, and but few days' dry provisions. Indeed, he tells us that he believes that no fleet was ever sent to sea in so poor a condition.

October 16th: They tell me in Westminster that there is never a doctor and only one apothecary* left, all being dead. There are great hopes of a great decrease this week. God send it!

October 31st: Thus we end the month merrily and all the more because, after some fears that the plague would have increased again this week, I hear for certain that there is more than 400 decrease, the whole number of deaths being 1,388 and of them, of the plague 1,031. Want of money in the Navy puts everything out of order. Men grow mutinous and no-one minds the business of the Navy but myself. I have great hopes of promotion to Surveyor General of Provisions, which would bring me £300 a year.

November 22nd: I heard today that Mr. Harrington is not dead of the plague as we believed. At which I was very glad, but most of all to hear that the plague has come very low, the total deaths less than 1,000, with plague 600 and great hopes of a further decrease, because of this day's being a very hard frost - and still freezing.

November 30th: Great joy we have this week in the weekly Bill, it being come to 544 in all and only 333 of the plague. My father writes, as great news for them, that he saw Yorke's wagon go up to London again this week, full of passengers. He tells me that my Aunt Bell has been dead of the plague for the last seven weeks.

LONDON'S BURNING!

Disease was not the only hazard of seventeenth century town
life. In small market towns and larger cities, ancient wooden
houses crowded closely together, roofed with dry thatch. Fires
were frequent and many towns like Bridgnorth, Dorchester,
Northampton and Warwick, were totally destroyed and rebuilt.
Samuel Pepys saw the most famous fire of all - before the war-
time Blitz - in 1666. Only one year after his long description
of the plague year, he reports another disaster in his daily diary.

1666: Sunday. September 2nd: Some of our maids were sitting
up late last night, to get things ready for our feast today. Jane
called us at about 3 in the morning, to tell us of a great fire they
saw in the City. So I got up and put on my nightgown* and went
to her window and thought the fire to be on the back side of Mark
Lane at the furthest. Being unused to such fires, I thought it was
far enough off for safety, and so went back to bed again and off to
sleep. About 7 o'clock, I got up again to dress myself and, looking
out of the window, saw the fire, not as much as it had been, and
further off. So to my new closet* to set things right after
yesterday's cleaning. By and by, Jane comes and tells me that she
heard that more than 300 houses were burned down last night by
the fire we saw, and that it was still burning all down Fish Street,
by London Bridge. ''

So, I made myself ready presently and walked to the Tower and
there got upon one of the high places, John Robinson's son going
up with me. There I saw the houses at that end of the bridge all
on fire, on this side and at the other end of the Bridge. This
troubled me for, amongst other people, poor little Mitchell and
our Sarah, on the Bridge. So down, with my heart full of trouble,
to the Lieutenant of the Tower, who tells me that it began this
morning in the King's baker's house in Pudding Lane and that it
has burned down St. Magnus's church and the greater part of Fish
Street already. Everybody was trying to remove their furniture,

flinging things into the River or bringing them into boats. I noticed that the poor pigeons were unwilling to leave their houses, but hovered around the windows and balconies until their wings were burned and they fell down.

At Whitehall, I went to the King's private room in his chapel, where many people came up to me and I gave them an account which upset them all. Word was taken in to the King and the Duke of York about what I had seen and that unless His Majesty ordered houses to be pulled down, nothing could stop the fire. The King ordered me to go to My Lord Mayor, with a message from him, to command him to spare no houses, but to pull them down in front of the Fire in all directions. The Duke of York told me to tell the Mayor that if he wanted more soldiers, he would have them. I walked along Watling Street as best I could, everybody was coming away, loaded with goods to save. Here and there were sick people carried away on their beds. Extraordinary valuable goods were being carried on carts and on people's backs. At last I met my Lord Mayor in Canning Street, like a man worn out, with a scarf around his neck. To the King's message, he cried, like a fainting woman: "Lord! What can I do? I am worn out! People will not obey me. I have been pulling down houses, but the fire overtakes us faster than we can do it." He said that he needed no more soldiers and that he must go and refresh himself, having been up all night. So, he left me and I walked home, seeing people frantic and nothing done to quench the fire. The houses too, very close together thereabouts, and full of stuff fit for burning, such as pitch and tar, warehouses of oil, wines and brandy and other inflammable goods. I saw the churches being filled with furniture, by people who themselves should have been quietly there at this time. Over all the Thames, with your face in the wind, you were almost burned by the shower of fire-drops. Houses caught fire from these flakes of fire, five or six houses at a time, one from another. The river was full of lighters* and boats, taking in goods, with valuable furniture floating in the water. I noticed that there was hardly one boat in three that had furniture which did not also have a pair of virginals* in it. When we could take no more on the water, we went to a little ale-house on Bankside and stayed there until it was almost dark and saw the fire grow. As it grew darker, it seemed more and more, in corners and on steeples, between churches and houses, as far as we could see up the hill of the City, in a most horrid, spiteful, blood-red flame, not like the fine flame of an ordinary fire. We stayed until we saw the fire as one whole arch of flame, from one side to the other of the Bridge and in a bow up the hill, an arch about a mile long. It made me weep to see it. Churches, houses and all were on fire, all flaming at once, with a horrid noise the flames made and the cracking of the houses in their ruin.

We went home with sore hearts, and poor Tom Hater came with some of his furniture, saved from his house which is burned down on Fish Street hill. I invited him to sleep at my house and took in his goods, but he never slept there. The noise of the growth of the fire coming nearer every moment, we were forced to begin to pack up our own goods and prepare for their removal. By moonlight we carried my furniture into the garden and Mr. Hater and I removed my money and iron chests into the cellar, thinking that the safest place. I got my bags of gold into my office, ready to carry away and buried my wines and cheeses in pits in the garden. We put Mr. Hater to bed for a while, poor man, but he got very little rest, as there was so much noise in my house, carrying out the furniture.

September 4th: After supper, I walked in the dark down to Tower Street, where begins the practice of blowing up houses near the Tower. At first this frightened people more than anything, but it stopped the fire wherever it was done, bringing the houses down where they stood, so that it was easy to quench whatever little fire was left in them. William Hewer went today to see how his mother was getting on. He came home late, telling us how he had been forced to move her to Islington, her house in Pie Corner being burned. So it has got as far as that and all the Old Bailey and running down into Fleet Street. St. Paul's is burned and all Cheapside. I wrote to my father tonight, but the post-house was burned and the letter could not go.

September 5th: I lay down in my office again, on Will Hewer's quilt, being very weary and sore in my feet with walking until I could hardly stand. About 2 in the morning, my wife calls me up and tells me of new cries of "Fire!", it having come to Barking Church, which is at the bottom of our lane. I got up and finding that this was so, decided immediately to take her away to safety. This I did, and took my gold, which was about £2,350, with Will Hewer and Jane, down by Pundy's boat to Woolwich. At Woolwich, when I came, I found the gates shut, but no guards kept at all. Which troubled me, because of rumours now begun, that there is a plot behind it and that the French have done it. I got the gates open and went to Mr. Sheldon's, where I locked up my gold and told my wife and Will Hewer never to leave the room together, without one or the other of them staying there, by day or night. I went home and though I expected to see our house on fire, it being now 7 o'clock, it was not. I was so sure that I would find our Office on fire that I dared not ask anyone how it was with us until I came to it, and found it not burned. I went to the top of Barking steeple and from there I saw the saddest sight of desolation that I ever saw. Everywhere, great fires. Oil cellars and brimstone and other things burning, I became afraid to stay there long and came down as fast as I could, the fire having spread as far as I could see. Then I went to Sir William Penn's and there ate a piece of cold meat, having eaten nothing since Sunday but the remains of our Sunday dinner. I lay down and slept a good night about midnight. When I got up, I heard that there had been a great alarm of French and Dutch invasion, which proved to be nothing. It is strange how long it seems since Sunday, having been always so full of a variety of actions and little sleep. It seems a week or more, I have almost forgotten what day it is.

LONDON'S BURNING!

THE EVIDENCE

The Narrator: Samuel Pepys (1633-1703) was a London tailor's son, educated at St. Paul's School and Cambridge. During the Commonwealth he was secretary to Lord Mountagu, one of Cromwell's young colonels, who became General at Sea. In 1656, Pepys became Clerk to the Exchequer and in 1660, when Mountagu turned in favour of Restoration, Pepys sailed to Holland with his master and escorted the King to England. His diary begins on January 1st., 1660, describing at first-hand, Charles II's return to England. He was rewarded with the post of Clerk to the Navy Board, with an official house at the Navy Office in Seething Lane (EC3), near St. Olave's church, where Pepys and his wife are buried. Pepys wrote his diaries in shorthand code, from 1660 to 1669, when failing eyesight prevented him from writing more. He gained promotion as Secretary to the Admiralty and was responsible for laying the foundations of a well organised Navy. His devotion to the ships and their officers shines through his writing, with a great deal of inside information. Pepys was an important civil servant, with access to the King and his brother, James Duke of York, (later James II), who also took a great interest in naval affairs. In 1673, Pepys was elected MP for Castle Rising in Norfolk, later for Harwich, in Essex. In 1678 the Duke of York was accused of organising a Catholic plot to overthrow the government. Pepys was arrested and sent to the Tower, but no charges were brought against him. With James II's accession, he returned to the Admiralty, but was again thrown out with the Catholic king in the Revolution of 1688. He spent his last years organising his library. Pepys's diaries were very private records of his daily life. They reveal a busy, conscientious man, with many human failings, but an acute sense of observation. He was ambitious, vain about his clothes, flirtatious and unfaithful to his young French wife. He was often bad-tempered and jealous but his ambitious self-seeking and greed for his gold are honestly stated. He was fond of music, the theatre and above all, of wine, food and good company. The diaries are a unique source of 17th century social history.

The Diaries: The original handwritten books are in the Pepys Library at Magdalene College, Cambridge. They were published in three major 19th century editions, firstly by Richard, Lord Braybrooke, in 1825; then by Rev. Mynors Bright in 1875-9; next, the most comprehensive early version, by H.B. Wheatley, in 10 volumes (1893-9). Our extracts are taken from Wheatley's edition. Teachers will find the fourth, complete and most authentic edition, edited by Robert Latham and William Matthews, as 11 volumes (1970-83), available in most reference libraries but, more convenient for purchase is the *Shorter Pepys,* a single volume abridged by Latham in 1986, and an *Illustrated Pepys* (1978).

Because editors have been faced by the problem of decoding Pepys's shorthand and expanding this into readable prose, every edition must be a reconstruction rather than an exact reproduction of what Pepys intended to write. Thus, Wheatley's edition is condemned for being "peppered with inaccuracies" and he is criticised because he "saw fit to smooth out the occasional rough edges of Pepys's prose." For the benefit of modern children, our own extracts have taken similar liberties with words and phrases, but the sense and content of Pepys's observations have not been tampered with.

CHECK THE EVIDENCE

Pepys certainly never intended that other people should read his private diaries and there was no intention that they would be published. What difference does this make to their evidence? Pepys was a fussy man. What effect was that likely to have upon those observations which you have read? Make a list of subjects which Pepys was best qualified to tell us about.

A diary will be even more private than letters such as Lady Brilliana's, which were intended to be read by another person. Beware, however, of those, like modern politicians, who write diaries with one eye on future publication. What happens in those cases?

LONDON'S BURNING!

Most writers say that Pepys was vain, ambitious, musical, kind-hearted, sometimes selfish but loyal and hardworking. Find any entries in our stories which support these judgements. Make lists of evidence for and against his character and come to your own decision.

Compare Pepys's account with the journals of Evelyn (1665) and Defoe (1722).

There are many easily available early maps and pictorial *Prospects* of seventeenth century London. Study these, to find the streets, buildings and other places which Pepys describes in his diaries.

Can you find Pepys's house or district on the Prospect of London? Make a graph of plague deaths from June 29th — November 30th.

INFORMATION

The Great Plague of 1665: The disease was bubonic plague which swept repeatedly through Europe for many centuries. The earlier Black Death produced accounts (see *TELLTALE TWO*) of a similar medieval epidemic, though leprosy was a more permanent health hazard at that time. (See too, how smallpox also claimed its victims in 1665 and how the Mortality Bill included hundreds of weekly non-plague fatalities.) All old towns were insanitary, overcrowded places, with no proper drainage, rubbish- or sewage-disposal. Modern London has similar problems! In 1603, 30,578 Londoners died of this horrible disease; 11,785 in 1610; 63,001 in 1625 and 23,359 in 1636. From June 1665 to February 1666, the death toll was 66,553 (but note Pepys's observation on the unreliability of statistics.) These figures were recorded in weekly Mortality Bills which were posted in the city. As the diary shows, the epidemic was at its peak in the hot weather of July to September, but lingered on throughout the winter of 1665-6.

The sickness was brought into England by infected rats and was spread by lice. These travelled in bales of cloth, wool and other goods, so that sea-ports, market towns and villages along trade-routes were especially open to plague. The *plague tokens* were buboes, swellings of glands in the armpits and groin. Other symptoms included fever, vomiting, a rash on the body and blue-black bruises on the legs. The disease struck very quickly, as Pepys's poor coachman discovered. Patients died within a week and there was only a 25% chance of recovery. There was little possibility of treatment for so many sick people at once, especially as doctors were at risk. People thought that the visitation was the result of sinfulness, which could be remedied only by prayer. Some people suspected a plot, by the Dutch, the Jews or Roman Catholics. (The same suspicions would be aroused by the Fire, next year.) Suggested precautions were tobacco, alcohol, astrology and magic charms. Medical treatment included blood-letting and medicines made of toads, snakes, powdered bone, chicken feathers, frogs' legs and plague-water made of urine and pepper. Pepys's "strong water" was probably brandy - or Navy rum! There was some understanding of the value of fresh air, isolation, sweating out the fever and diligent care of the sick by brave, unknown men and women.

There were only three seventeenth century London Hospitals: St. Thomas's in Southwark, St. Bartholomew's in Smithfield and St. Mary's Bethlehem or Bedlam, now the Imperial War Museum. These became so full that doctors and nurses had to walk over the beds, there was no room between them. Meanwhile doctors and clergymen died, churches were closed, servants were dismissed and graveyards filled. As Pepys pointed out, many of the rich and famous inhabitants, including the Royal family, left London for safety in the countryside. Many others, officials like Pepys, apothecaries and physicians, stayed on to cope with everyday life in London. The Lord Mayor and Council made valiant efforts to cope with the disaster. *Pest-houses* were set up as isolation hospitals at Westminster, Soho, Stepney, and Marylebone. *Orders for Health* were issued and local officials were appointed, Examiners, Nurses, Searchers and Corpse-bearers. Infected houses were sealed up and marked with a red cross. Cats and dogs were destroyed (an unwise move in view of the danger from rats), and an effort was made to cleanse the streets. Plague victims were collected by carts and buried by night in plague-pits, sometimes only a few inches below ground. Soon these too became full and corpses were stacked by the roadside. A relic of the plague is the nursery rhyme, *Ring-a-ring o'roses*. Roses are the rash, the rings are round, inflamed patches or plague-tokens and posies were sniffed to avoid the unhealthy stench. Sneezing, giddiness and falling down were also symptoms.

The Great Fire of 1666: The fire began in Farriners, the king's baker's shop in Pudding Lane near Eastcheap (EC3). It ended, three days later, at Pie Corner on Cock Lane (EC1) where a gilt cherub marks the spot. The baker and his family escaped over the roof-tops, but their maid-servant was burned to death. At first, the Mayor and parish constables ignored the fire, but by morning it was out of control. In all, nearly 400 acres within the City walls were totally destroyed, including 87 churches and 13,200 houses. Only 83 acres outside the walls were affected and it is a remarkable fact that only 9 people died. Refugees camped in tents outside the City; rumours of a foreign plot spread rapidly. These were denied publicly by Charles II, but a Frenchman confessed (!) to having set fire to the baker's shop and was hanged at Tyburn. New Government offices and law courts were set up to restore law and order. Rebuilding was prohibited until plans had been made for clearing the debris, establishing a new building-line, planning stone-built houses and less overcrowded streets. Ambitious plans for a less crowded, quieter City, proposed by Evelyn and Wren, were dismissed as not being convenient to trade. Measures were taken to improve drainage, water supply and street-cleaning and a coal tax was levied to provide money for public buildings. By 1672 most of the rebuilding of private houses, Guildhall and churches was complete. Wren's Monument on Fish Street Hill, EC3, built in 1672, commemorates the Fire. It is 61.5m high, the same as the distance eastward from its base to the spot where the Fire broke out.

LONDON'S BURNING!

WHAT IS YOUR VERDICT?

It is easy for modern people to be contemptuous of our ancestors' standards and the scale of their disasters. It is very easy too, to point out the many hazards which their towns produced. How much have we improved our own conditions of life? Check statistics, for example, of coastline pollution, nuclear disasters, road deaths, lung cancer, lethal foam-filled furniture, dangerous football terraces, alcoholism and Aids, to discover just how much we have improved.

Tragically, national disasters still occur quite regularly. Keep records of these and compare modern emergency services, rescue operations and remedies with those available to the Mayor in 1666.

Does Pepys's diary give the impression of a brave man? What opinion do you form of King Charles II?

Notice how often in our stories of disasters, we shall find rumours of plots and the demand for scapegoats - usually innocent immigrants. Notice too, the ability to produce victims for confession and punishment. Make your own comparisons with modern times.

From the clues he offers about himself, write your own description of the sort of man you think he was. Draw a picture of the man you imagine, then ask to see a contemporary likeness. Is our own portrait reliable? (See portrait on p. 122.)

THE YOUNG SEA-CAPTAIN

Every lifetime is a complete story, with a beginning, a middle and an end. The evidence which tells that story is more like a jigsaw puzzle, made up piece by piece. Given fragments of evidence, can you put the puzzle together, after 300 years? Here is the story of a fifteen-year-old boy from Worcestershire, who went to sea in 1693. After many adventures, he was promoted Captain of his own small frigate*, sailed with Benbow to the West Indies, and patrolled on war-time service against French privateers* in the English Channel. His name was Edmund Lechmere, Ned to his friends, and this is his story. It is taken from the letters he wrote, as a boy, to his family, and, as a young sea-Captain, to the Admiralty. We begin the story, as so often happens, at the end. Here is a letter, written by two young naval officers, which breaks the news of their Captain's death to his older brother.

Aboard HMS Lyme at Plymouth   **January 16th. 1704**
To Nicholas Lechmere Esq., in Hare Court, Temple, London.

Sir, Its an unpleasant task, that the first and only business we have with a Gentleman of your worth and character should be to give an account of your brother's death. His uncommon gallantry has completed his period of service sooner than might have been expected from his age and good health.

In our return from a cruise to the westward in Her Majesty's ship the *Lyme,* having several ships under his convoy, a French privateer of 46 guns fell in with his fleet. The Captain saw them safely into harbour, then pursued the Enemy, who gave him battle. Being close aboard each other, he first had the misfortune to be wounded in both knees, which forced him to call for a chair. Through the great zeal* he had to do his Duty in the best manner, he raised himself to look over the side. In that fatal moment he received a musket shot that passed through his body.

This happened yesterday, and he arrived at this place in the night. Mr. Young an eminent* surgeon was sent to him and seemed to have some hope for him, but, his wound bleeding inwardly, he died this morning about 9 o'clock, to the great grief of all who knew him. On this sad occasion, you have, with all his relations, the satisfaction of his having departed from this life with as much gallantry as anyone ever left it. So many good things are said about him by his officers that, in the midst of sorrow for the loss of such a man, we have occasion to rejoice at his great courage.

Sir, your most humble servants

John Struley and John Holmes

How did this sad loss come about? Let us gather together a few of the jigsaw puzzle pieces. The Key to the evidence and the date of each piece is given later. The first piece is dated:

1: **Sunday April 22nd. 1677**: About 11 at night, my daughter-in-law Mrs. Lucy Lechmere was delivered of a son at my house at Hanley. He was named Edmund, after the names of his father, great-grandfather and grandfather's grandfather. *Bendicat Deus.** *Amen.*

2: Madam: What I proposed to Baron Lechmere was the sending of one of your sons as a Volunteer to sea. This scheme was designed as an encouragement for gentlemen of quality to send their sons to sea so that, besides seamen's wages and victuals* the King allows them £24 a year. Their parents usually pay this money to the Captain, for eating at his table. The Captain has particular care of their education. This is a much better way for any young gentleman to come to preferment* than that of putting them as apprentices to merchant captains. If they do their duty there is no question of them making their fortunes. If you approve of this, I would advise sending him to London at the first

THE SECTION OF A FIRST RATE SHIP : CIRCA 1700

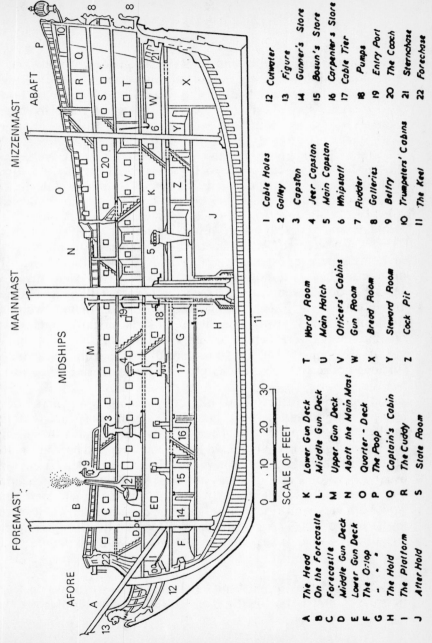

SCALE OF FEET

0 10 20 30

A The Head
B On the Forecastle
C Forecastle
D Middle Gun Deck
E Lower Gun Deck
F The Orlop
G " " "
H The Hold
I The Platform
J After Hold

K Lower Gun Deck
L Middle Gun Deck
M Upper Gun Deck
N Abaft the Main Mast
O Quarter - Deck
P The Poop
Q Captain's Cabin
R The Cuddy
S State Room

T Ward Room
U Main Hatch
V Officers' Cabins
W Gun Room
X Bread Room
Y Steward Room
Z Cock Pit

1 Cable Holes
2 Galley
3 Capstan
4 Jeer Capstan
5 Main Capstan
6 Whipstall
7 Rudder
8 Galleries
9 Belfry
10 Trumpeters' Cabins
11 The Keel

12 Cutwater
13 Figure
14 Gunner's Store
15 Bosun's Store
16 Carpenter's Store
17 Cable Tier
18 Pumps
19 Entry Port
20 The Coach
21 Sternchase
22 Forechase

opportunity, and sending him to Mr. Flamstead at Greenwich, to learn Navigation for three or four months, after which I will take care to have him put on board a ship where he shall have a Captain who will take special care of him. If he does not come to preferment, it will be his own fault.

3:    Dear Sister Lucy: To give an account of my travels.   On Wednesday last we came safe to London. On Thursday, we dined with my Aunt Montague, on Friday with Sir James James at a Tavern, on Saturday with my cousin Richard Lechmere aboard ship, on Sunday with my uncle Hungerford, the Colonel, on Monday and Tuesday with my Grandfather in his chambers. Yesterday I went to Westminster Abbey, and saw the monuments of famous people, especially General Monk and King Charles II, dressed in their own clothes and seeming as if they were alive. In the afternoon I went to the Tower and saw six lions, the King's crown and many other strange things.   After that, I went to Bedlam*, where I saw mad people of all sorts, singing, dancing and reading. Some were as mad as Sister Pen is, when she is in one of her fits of temper. Tell her to be careful, for Bedlam is a wonderful large house and room enough for her if she doesn't take care.

4:    Honoured Mother: You asked me the hours of our school's lessons, which are not fixed, but Mr. Coulson takes care that the smaller boys are punctual. There are two other boys living with the family beside myself and we live in one room. There are many other mad fellows, but we have nothing to do with them. We usually have one dish of meat amongst so many hungry seamen and it amazed me, when I first came, to see so much snatching. Now I am very well skilled at it, and can help myself. The time of my going to sea is uncertain yet. People tell me of the great dangers of going to sea, but as for that, I will put my faith in Providence.

5:    This is the last opportunity I shall have to write to you from London. On Monday night's tide, I go aboard Captain Galloway's ship at Gravesend and so to the Downs*. The Monk has lain there this last three months and has taken some prizes*.

6:    Honoured Sir: This day I received your letter and give thanks for my sword, which I have not yet received. I understand that it will not be convenient to send me a silver-hilted sword, which I hope I can manage without. Our ship is a third rate, but a very small one, we carry only 54 guns and our number of men is not complete. The convoy is only 14 English and 8 Dutchmen, which is very weak to oppose the French Toulon Fleet.

7:    I suppose that you have heard the bad news of our fleet, but especially about our ship, the *Monk,* which, I hear the news in England is that she is lost, but thanks to God we are as safe as any of His Majesty's ships, though we have faced more dangers than any other ship in the Fleet. We were left alone and scattered from our company for a matter of a week, but by good Providence at the Island of Madeira, the first port we put into, we met with Sir George Rooke with about 55 sail of ships.

8:    The Virginny* Fleet is safely arrived in this Road*, and we have impressed* nearly 50 men from out of their ships. I have enquired all about the Fleet for a flying squirrel, but they brought none over with them this time. I have got as good a present for you, a couple of red birds from Virginny, the finest creatures you ever saw, all over as red as blood. They sing finely and will learn anything. I can get them safely to London, if you can arrange to get them to Hanley.

9:    I can now send you word that I have been in an engagement by sea. Yesterday a ship appeared which was thought to be a Frenchman by Sir George Rooke, who was on board us. He sent out some boats from the Fleet to fight her, armed with muskets and cutlasses. I went in one of the boats with one of our Lieu-tenants and when we came up to her, she hoisted French colours. We engaged her for about half an hour and she, seeing the others boats coming up struck* her flag and cried out for quarter*. Being a privateer, she had nothing but provisions and arms aboard, therefore there was little or no plunder. We had not one man wounded, though the shot flew very thick.

10: Fresh gales. At 7 this morning, we made the signal to un-moor and at 11 weighed* anchor in company with the *Falmouth, Lynn* and *Dunkirk,* bound for the West Indies, with Colonel Collingwood's Regiment on board.

11: December 2nd. 1698: Whitehall to Lord Ambassador Williamson: We have a report from Falmouth that on Tuesday afternoon, Rear Admiral Benbow sailed from St. Helen's in HMS *Gloucester,* with the *Falmouth, Lynn, Dunkirk* etc., bound for the West Indies. They have on board Col. Collingwood's Regiment, which they are to land on the Leeward Islands.

12: At noon the wind shifted and blew hard. The *Lynn* lost her main topsail..... Very stormy weather and a great sea. At 7, the *Dunkirk* sprung* her mainmast between decks. We bore down to her, upon her making the signal of being in distress. We sail much better than any ship in this company.

13: At one in the morning the tie of our main topsail yard halyards* gave way, and, the yards coming down, broke our main topgallant* yard. At 4 we got a new one up.

14: At one in the morning we brought to and at 4 made sail, imagining ourselves to be near the land. As soon as it was light, we found the Island of Barbados within a league. At 9 in the morning, we anchored in Carlisle Bay, where a great many merchant ships were riding. They saluted us, as also did the forts, with 21 guns. Total distance, from Madeira, 907 leagues*.

15: The charts have this coast false in every respect, we being wholly unacquainted here. We made out a high hill, with a monastery on the top, which proved to be Cartagena. We hoisted a Union Flag at mizzen topmast head. The people of the country fired their alarm guns along shore and a sloop* came out to view us. Here we could not be supplied with water. We stood in the passage, which is very narrow, but the Spaniards would not admit us into the harbour. Just within the harbour mouth there is a fort, with about 20 guns mounted.

16: From Mr. William Beeston in Jamaica, to Mr. Secretary Vernon: We begin to be infested with pirates and, to add to their number, a vessel which came from New York and was cleaned has turned rogue and captured ships on this coast of Hispaniola. On 23rd. January the *Falmouth* and *Lynn* arrived here. Rear Admiral Benbow left them at Nevis and ordered them to come on here.

17: Three deserters condemned to die. By favour of the court, they were allowed to throw dice for their lives - one to die, the others to be whipped from ship to ship, with halters around their necks.

18: This morning Captain Townsend of His Majesty's ship the *Lynn* died. The ship's colours half-staff up and fired 20 guns by the half-minute glass. This day Admiral Benbow gave me a commission to command the *Lynn*.

19: Off Porto Bello: In the evening a Portuguese sloop* arrived with Negroes from Cartagena. Our boats brought her down to the Admiral, at which the fort fired several times. The Admiral detained two priests out of her, in lieu* of some Englishmen they had taken prisoner, and sent the vessel into the Port.

20: Squally weather with much rain and tornadoes. Two of our men died; almost all the ship's company is violently sick. Only seven men in a watch are well.

21: Endeavouring to get into Porto Bello. Many Tornadoes and much rain. Two of our men died this day and none are recovered yet. The *Falmouth* so sickly that they could not get her anchor up without my help. My people are somewhat recovered.

22: Kidd, the famous pirate, is about the islands. In Runaway Bay, so called because deserted slaves settled there, we took charge of a merchantman whose Captain had broken orders and stolen his ship and cargo on the account of piracy.

23: Sancta Martha: Here for the nourishment of my weak men, I victualled* with fresh beef, which is plentiful and very cheap, also much wild fowl here. Several gold mines lie within a few leagues of this place, but the slothfulness* of the Spaniards will not allow them to labour there. Three ships arrived, one from Barbados and a Guinea merchant with negroes. At this time they are at a very great price, worth £35 apiece to the planters.

24: Weighed anchor from Port Royal. Homeward bound.

25: I made the best of my way up the Channel. At 8 at night close off Portland, made an easy sail and at 5 anchored at St. Helens, near Rear Admiral Benbow, who arrived here last night. I gave account of my arrival to My Lords of the Admiralty. We had orders not to cast off any boat, nor allow our people to go ashore, they being fearful of an infection from the West Indies.

26: The *Lynn* wanting repair in her upper work, I was commissioned as Captain of the *Lyme,* she being fit for the sea. My officers and company also removed with me.

27: Sir: On 23rd of this month I met with two French privateers, with a prize being a pink* of 200 tons, laden with sugar from the West Indies, off Lands End. I recaptured the pink and took one of the privateers, which I ordered into Plymouth. On 21st, the *Medway* and I met with a French ship of 40-50 guns, but in the night he made his escape and another of 20 guns with him.

28: Honoured Sir, In the company of the *Dragon, Hector, Mermain* and *Griffin Fireship*, I sailed with the Newfoundland Fleet and New England Fleets as far westward as 150 leagues from Scilly, then parted from them. In plying* between there and Cape Clear we saw only two French privateers of about 24 and 16 guns, which we could not come up with, our ships being very foul. On 17th a very hard storm blew us off that station to 35 leagues off Scilly. Between there and here we have chased 3 privateers, but at different times, so that it may be the same ship. We have not met with any merchant ships, but much bad weather.

29: I beg the favour that you will be pleased to let His Highness know of my application for a 4th. Rate ship. I have now commanded a 5th Rate almost 5 years and, having been on duty abroad since the war, have probably missed the opportunity of promotion. All my juniors on the List have the command of 4th. Rates.

30: Sir, Being under sail going out, the Masters of 6 or 7 small coasters laden with charcoal for the tin mines, bound to Falmouth, make their application to go under my convoy. I have thought fit to take them with me.

31: Plymouth, January 16th: Yesterday the *Lyme* frigate came in here, having left the Grand Fleet on Wednesday last 80 leagues West of Scilly. On her return she engaged a French man-of-war of 46 guns for 3 hours. During the engagement the *Lyme* had 24 men killed and the Captain mortally wounded, who died this morning.

32: Near this place is buried the Body of Captain Edmund Lechmere, formerly Commander of Her Majesty's Ship *Lynn* and late of the *Lyme,* a Frigate of 32 guns. On board of which he departed this life the sixteenth of January 1704.

THE EVIDENCE

The Documents: The Lechmere family papers are kept at the CRO in Worcester, with Ned's log-books. His letters, as a Captain, to the Admiralty, are found at the Public Record Office in London. The full story was published in *A Captain in the Navy of Queen Anne,* by John West (Longman's *Then & There series,* 1970), but this is now out of print. These extracts, brief fragments from more than 100 original documents, tell a much abridged version of the story :-

1: Diary of Sir Nicholas Lechmere for Sunday, April 22nd, 1677:

2: Letter from Anthony Cary, Lord Falkand, Treasurer to the Navy, to his aunt, Mrs. Lucy Lechmere. May 31st, 1692.

3-5: Letters from Edmund Lechmere to his sister Lucy, mother and grandfather, from London. June 14th - December 31st, 1692.

6 & 7: Letters from Edmund Lechmere to his grandfather, from aboard the *Monk* at Spithead. February 27th and August 8th, 1693.

8 & 9: Letters from Edmund Lechmere to his mother, from the *Grafton* in the Downs, March 28th and April 18th, 1694.

10: Entry in the log-book of HMS *Gloucester* for 29th. November, 1698.

11: Extract from the *Calendar of State Papers,* 1698.

12-15: Daily entries from the logbook of the *Gloucester* from December 2nd, 1698 to 23rd. January 1699, including voyage to the West Indies.

16: Official letter from the *Calendar of State Papers,* 1699.

17&18: Daily entries from the logbook of the *Gloucester* for March 2nd and March 12th, 1699.

19-23: Daily entries from the Captain's logbook of the *Lynn,* in the West Indies, from March 28th to October 22nd, 1699.

24&25: Daily entries from the logbook of the *Lynn* for February 29th to June 29th, 1700. Homeward voyage from the West Indies.

26: Daily entry from the logbook of the *Lynn* for 27th. November, 1701.

27-30: Letters from *HMS Lyme* to Admiralty, July 24th, 1703 to January 5th 1704. On duty in the Channel and N Atlantic

31: Front page of *The Flying Post* of Thursday, January 20th 1704.

32: Part of the inscription of a memorial in St. Andrew's Church, Plymouth.

CHECK THE EVIDENCE

You have several different kinds of documents here, both private and official. Study the differences in the information each type offers you. Which is the most neutral document? Which type is most informative? Check the evidence for any signs of boasting or exaggeration.

Notice the written style of the letters. How does the manner of addressing family and superior officers vary from modern fashions?

There are two ways of using the extracts. Either they can simply be told, from beginning to end, as a complete story, or used literally as a jigsaw puzzle. In the latter case, photocopy the extracts and cut them up into their numbered pieces. Black out the numbers. Shuffle the paper slips and you now have the mass of unsorted evidence, just as you would find it in different batches at the various repositories. Now see if you can sort the evidence into a chronological order.

Your teacher will write the four sources of information (family papers, ships' log books, official letters and public prints - newspaper and memorial) on the blackboard. First of all, see if you can identify the source of each extract. You may find it easier to do this work in groups - one group for log books, one for family papers, one for each ship. The sorting then becomes a Happy Families game, putting each each set of sources in order to make the correct chronological sequence. Check your sequence with the Key.

INFORMATION

Judge Nicholas Lechmere (1613-1701): Edmund's paternal grandfather, was a well-known Parliamentarian and a strict Puritan, of a similar family to the Harleys of Brampton. His diary tells a great deal about War years, when Royalist troopers stabled their horses in his grounds at Hanley Castle and threatened to kill his family because he had joined Parliament's army. The first and last battles of the War were fought at Powicke Bridge, outside the city of Worcester and near the Lechmeres' house. The Judge supported Cromwell and the Commonwealth but obtained a pardon and retired when Charles II was restored in 1660. (He went through his diary and carefully blacked out any insulting words about the Royalists). The Judge was fond of his son's wife, Mrs. Lucy Lechmere and she had a great affection for him. Ned was a favourite grandson; Sir Nicholas gave him his first naval sword (and strawberries for tea when he was a boy) and left him his silver tankard and loving message in his will.

The Glorious Revolution of 1688, which brought William III and Parliament to power, was favourable to the Judge's politics. He was made a Baron of the Exchequer and a member of the House of Lords. His diary describes his son's wedding day and mentions that Anthony Cary, Lucy Lechmere's nephew, later an incompetent Treasurer to the Navy, was amongst the wedding guests. Sir Nicholas was buried in Hanley church in no coffin, but a Puritan's woollen shroud. Mrs. Lechmere completed his diary with a note of "My worthy, good father-in-law's death on April 30th, 1701. He was a man of great piety and learning, and kind to all".

William III (1688-1702): was king throughout Ned's short life-time. A Dutchman and a fierce opponent of the French king, he was offered the throne with, and on behalf of his wife, Queen Mary II (1688-1694), daughter of Princess Mary Stuart, thus Charles I's grand-daughter. The joint monarchy was chosen by Parliament in their final victory over the Stuarts, with the enforced abdication of Charles II's brother, James II. (Pepys's Duke of York). The new monarchs were staunch Protestants, prepared to rule within Parliament's terms of reference. William 'The Deliverer' was a keen naval supporter - the Gentleman Volunteers' scheme under which Edmund joined the Navy was the King's own idea. The Dutch fleet too, was a welcome addition to the English navy. In Pepys's time they had been England's most persistent - often victorious - naval adversary. Lechmere continually mentions actions in which Dutch and English ships sailed together and there are several logbook entries about royal visits to the fleet.

War with France: For many reasons, England turned to war with France as a result of our alliance with Holland. France's support of the exiled Stuarts involved continual possibility of French invasion. France, under Louis XIV, also replaced Spain as our chief commercial and colonial rival. Before, during and after Edmund Lechmere's naval service, England and France were at

war in two phases, from 1688 to 1713, including the first out-
breaks of colonial wars in America, India and the West Indies. At
sea, the French were at first victorious in several confused naval
actions, similar to that described by Ned in Letter 7. Gradually
however, William III's ships gained the upper hand and, by 1692
the French battle fleet was decisively defeated at a time when
Louis XIV could no longer afford its upkeep. The Frenchmen
then turned to privateering, licensed piracy which attacked British
merchant shipping in the same way as U-boat campaigns of World
Wars I and II.

Admiral John Benbow (1653-1702): was born in Shrewsbury.
Apprenticed to a butcher, he ran away to sea and became a
master's mate in 1678. He was a *tarpaulin* officer, risen from the
ranks to chase pirates off Tangier. When Ned joined the Navy,
Benbow was Rear Admiral, commander of the squadron in the
West Indies. There is no doubt that Benbow was a hero to young
Ned. In 1702 off the Indies, he fought for four days against a
superior French force and his right leg was shattered by chain
shot*. The Captains of the ships in his squadron deserted him, but
the Admiral called for a chair to be brought to the quarter deck so
that he could direct the action more closely. He was taken to
Jamaica, where, before he died, he had the runaway Captains
court-martialled and hanged. A contemporary folk song tells of
how "Brave Benbow lost his legs by chain shot". This story
undoubtedly influenced Ned Lechmere's last action.

The Ships: Seventeenth century men-of-war were rated, from
First to Sixth Rate ships of the Line of Battle. The rating
depended upon size, armament and number of crew, from 100-gun
First Rates to 24-gun Sixths. The seven ships in which Ned served
were:-

Monk: (Jan:1692 - Oct:1693) Third Rate: 60 guns, Length 136ft,
340 men. Captain Fairbourne: *Grafton:* (March: 1694 - Sept:
1695) Third Rate: 70 guns, Length 15ft, 460 men: *Burford:*

(March: 1696 - June: 1696) Third Rate: 70 guns, Length 150ft, 460 men. Captain Fitzpatrick: *Royal Katherine:* (June: 1696 - Oct: 1697) Second Rate: 84 guns, Length 153ft. 540 men. Captains Gothar and Pickard: *Gloucester:* Oct: 1697 - March: 1699) Fourth Rate: 60 guns, Length 145ft. 346 men: *Lynn:* (March: 1699 - May: 1702) Fifth Rate: 32 guns, Length 109ft. 135 men. Captains Townsend and Lechmere: *Lyme:* (May: 1702 - Jan: 1704) Fifth Rate: 32 guns, Length 109ft. 145 men. Captain Lechmere.

Resources: The **National Maritime Museum**, Romney Road, Greenwich, London SE10 9NF (01 858 4422) holds thousands of valuable documents, pictures and models which illustrate the history of the Navy. For Ned's service, these include: log-books; ships draughts, plans and elevations; muster books or registers of the ships' crews, from Captain to ships' carpenters and cabin boys; charts and navigation instruments; biographies of both naval officers and ships; ships' models and pictures of these; paintings of Admirals and naval actions and pictures of these in slides and post-cards.

Also at Greenwich are the shipwright Keltridge's plans or drafts of each of the Rates of naval ships. Simplified, the Fifth Rate draft can be used to make a model of the *Lyme*.

The Public Record Office, Chancery Lane, London WC2A 1LR (071 405 3488) holds the Admiralty papers.

The Science Museum, Exhibition Road, London SW7 2DD (017 589 3456) also has many ships' models. These include a model of a Fifth rate of the same establishment as the *Lynn* and *Lyme*.

For other maritime museums, see *CLASSROOM MUSEUM,* by John West (ELM Publications,1990).

See: Nicholas Rodger's *Naval Records for Genealogists* (HMSO 1988)

WHAT IS YOUR VERDICT?

What sort of man emerges from the jigsaw puzzle? Does Edmund Lechmere seem to change at all from 1692 to 1704? Lord Falkland recommended William III's naval volunteers' entry scheme with high hopes of Edmund becoming an Admiral and making a fortune. He was 15 when he joined and 27 when he died; was he a failure?

There are many differences in methods of promotion and patronage (or favouritism) among the ruling classes of the seventeenth century, compared with our own system of qualifications for any job. The idea of *preferment* was very important to people of that period. How does it compare with modern equal opportunities? Check the meaning of the word nepotism* - does this apply to the Lechmere family?

In his letters to the Admiralty, did Ned claim any advantage from his family connections? What grounds did he give for expecting command of a larger ship than the *Lyme*? Do you think that he deserved promotion?

In all the stories in this book, from 1536 to 1704, you have seen many aspects of the behaviour and attitudes of people of those times. In what ways did they differ from ourselves? Were they in any way similar? In making your comparisons, pay particular attention to kindness, courtesy, hypocrisy, ambition, courage, tolerance, snobbery, sense of duty, cruelty and family affection.

Are we superior to our ancestors in our own concern for human rights, equal opportunities, free speech and careful government? Are we more, or less, hypocritical? What are the failings of modern humane behaviour.

accord	agreement
apothecary	chemist-physician, shopkeeper or druggist
apprentice	young person undergoing employment training
Articles	items, list of reforms
assone	as soon
Austin friar	Augustinian order
bark	barke, barque, any small sailing vessel
Bedlam	Bethlehem Hospital for the mentally ill
Belial	fallen angel, spirit of evil
Bendicat Deus	God's blessing
Bill	list, order or law
biscuit	hard ship's bread
bravoes	bullies, hooligans
broadpieces	a 20 shilling coin of silver (= £1.00)
buccaneers	pirates, especially on Spanish Main
bushel	measure of 8 gallons or about 2,200 cu.ins
camelot	camlet, Eastern velvet fabric
Candlemas	church festival on February 2nd
cannonading	bombarding with cannon-fire
catches	popular songs or choruses
chain shot	two cannon-balls, joined by chain
charged	ordered, given a duty or job to do
closet	large cupboard or small dressing-room
commonwealth	the people's good or welfare, the country
cope	ecclesiastical cape or robe
country	used in 17th century as county
CRO	County Record Office
crown	coin of value of ¼ of £1
cuirass	body armour, originally leather, breast-plate and back-plate to waist
cuirassiers	a horse-soldier, wearing a cuirass
dhows	single masted trading vessel of Indian Ocean and Red Sea
dragoons	mounted infantryman, armed with carbine
Downs	anchorage on E. coast inside Goodwin Sands
ducats	gold or silver coin
ell	length of 45 inches or 1,114mm
eminent	famous, well-qualified
Ensign	junior officer
entailed	left in trust to heirs
enthusiasm	fanaticism, unhealthy excitement
factories	warehouses, trading station
faggots	bundles of firewood, kindling
fanfaroons	bragging, swagger, exaggeration
ferrandin	farandine, fabric of silk and wool
fired	burned
flagship	carries the Admiral and his flag

fly-boat	flat-bottomed Dutch vessel, coastal use
forecastle	raised fore-cabin, crew's quarters
fowler	poultry merchant, gamekeeper
Foxhall	Vauxhall pleasure gardens on Surrey side of Thames, laid out in Charles II's reign
frigate	small three-masted ship of 5-6th rate
galleasses	combination of oars and sail, triangular (lateen) sails. Unsuitable as warships
galleons	ship with low forecastle, developed by Hawkins and used by Spaniards as merchants.
galleys	oared fighting ship, rowed by 100 slaves
gibbet	gallows
graved	careened, cleaned, weeds burned and scraped from ship's bottom
hackney-coach	4 wheeler, two horses, 6 seats for hire
half a crown	crown=¼ of £1, coin for 'half a crown' = 2s6d (12½ p)
halyards	ropes or tackle to hoist sails to yards
harness	armour
heretic	enemy of the Catholic faith, heathen
hulks	old ships, grounded, dismasted and used as house-boats or prisons
hundredweight	112lbs or 51kg
Infanta	Spanish princess, usually eldest daughter
in lieu of	instead of, in place of
invalid	useless, not in use
junks	Chinese flat-bottomed, three masted boat with four-sided lugsails of matting.
leagues	about 3 miles
leeward	pronounced loo-ard; down-wind
letters patent	royal order or monopoly
lieu	see in lieu of
luff	bringing ship closer to wind
lighters	barge or cargo-ship without sails
mainland	continuous shore, not an island
malignants	vicious people, Roundhead name for royalists
Mammon	the idol of greed
mariners	sailors
martial	warlike, military
match	slow-burning fuse
matins	midnight or daybreak service
militia	local Home Guard or muster
mitre	bishop's hat
mizzenmast	the third, aftermost mast
Moors	Muslims

Mortality Bill	weekly list of dead
mun	must (Scottish accent)
mystery	craft, trade or gild
nepotism	giving jobs to relatives
nightgown	dressing gown
paleography	ancient hand-writing
pataches	another name for pinnace
periwig	high, curled wig, with centre parting
pillory	wooden post for prisoners' neck and wrists
pink	small, square-rigged ship
pinnace	small ship of 20 tons; two masts and oars, used as messenger.
planted	set down, colonised
pocket borough	Parliament constituency owned by landlord
Pomfrett	town of Pontefract (Yorks.)
poop-castle	enclosure under poop deck, master's cabin
poop-deck	short, aftermost deck, above quarter-deck
prebend	canon of a cathedral, pension or living
preferment	promotion, advancement
privateers	small private warships, licensed to fight
prize	captured ship, value shared as prize-money
proclamation	announcement, edict or order
proscribed	condemned, banished, outlawed
quarter-deck	upper deck, aft of mainmast, commanded by Captain. Early bridge.
ranting	preaching, raving
reals de plata	royals, Spanish silver coins, larger ones were pieces of eight
recusants	secret Catholics
resolved	decided, vowed
rifled	ransacked, plundered
Road	sea-way, channel
Rump	the remains of the Long Parliament, after dismissal of moderate members.
sail	used to mean a ship - 'three sail of ships'
set his hand	made a signature, signed
Seven hills	Rome, the Papacy
shallops	small fishing vessel, 25 tuns, single mast
sheered off	sailed away, ran off
sheets	ropes or rigging
sloop	single-masted vessel or cutter
slothfulness	idleness, laziness
sprung	cracked or broken loose
Stannaries	special Court or Gild of Cornish tin-mines
stay	standing rigging, supporting mast
struck	hauled down (sail or flag)
swarthy	dark-skinned, temper, mood, attitude

thrush	disease, inflammation of mouth
topgallant	extra topmost mast and sails
touchwood	tinder
trice	instant, moment
tunnage	measurement of ship's loading capacity
Upper House	of Parliament, House of Lords
vanguard	ships in front
victual, to	to take on provisions
victuals	food, provisions
Viceroy	deputy of king
viols	musical instrument, like violin
virginals	keyboard instrument, set in a box, no legs
wainscote	wall-panelling
ward	walled area or yard
watermen	ferry-men
weigh	to lift the anchor
whipstaff	long steering pole, extension from rudder
zeal	enthusiasm
zealot	fanatic, enthusiastic supporter

APPENDIX A : CRITERIA FOR CHECKING THE EVIDENCE

Each of our stories has its own set of pertinent questions to challenge the evidence. Here are more general questions which can be copied as cue-cards for children's use, to test other stories. These are not intended to be used all at once! Obviously a set of questions - not more than four or five, and only one question to each card - will be selected as more apt to a particular story. These are more objective than the later **Verdict** discussion points.

1: The Narrator: Who was the narrator? What do we know about him/her? Is he/she a famous character in History books? Is it the Narrator's own story? Was he/she an eye-witness of the events described? Was the Narrator anywhere near the action? Did the Narrator live at the same time as the events, or later? How much later? Does he give any idea of where and how he found the information? Is his version copied from another account? Was this information first-hand, second-hand, or very old-hand? Do we know more about what happened at the time than the Narrator could have done? Who sees more of the game - players or spectators? Did the Narrator have any special reason for telling the story? Had he any special qualifications to know about the events? For example, if it was a battle, was he a soldier, etc? What does the Narrator think of the chief characters in the story? Is he trying to prove something by telling it? Is he in any way an official recorder of the events? Did he stand to profit from telling the story?

2: The Narrator's style: Is the story told clearly, without any muddle? Does the Narrator seem to exaggerate? Is he boastful, or modest? Is he likely to be biased- does he take sides? Does he tell the story angrily or calmly? Does he use technical language? Is there a moral to his tale? Does he always seem aware of his audience?

3. The facts: Is this the only version of the story? Can we list the facts that the Narrator gives us? Can we cross-check those facts with any other version? Is there any difference between his facts and his opinions? Are there any important details which seem to be missing? Are there any obvious mistakes or untruths? Is there anything in the story which you cannot believe?

4: The Action: Is the story true? Would you describe it as fact or fiction? Is it a myth or legend, a poem or a ballad? Could you make a collection of stories of the same type? If you were the Narrator, would you tell the story differently?

5: Matching different kinds of Evidence : Find pictures, poems, ballads, coins, archaeological remains, buildings and museum objects which relate to the different versions of the written evidence. Group them together and see if they all seem to tell the same story.

APPENDIX B : CRITERIA FOR 'VERDICT' QUESTIONS

These are more subjective than the Evidence questions and it is important that they do not become a blunt cross-questioning for didactic right-or-wrong answers. They are intended as the basis for discussion, debate and role-play. The main question should always be broken down and approached gradually by means of a series of directional sequences, leading towards the main issue. The questions should be interpreted as openly as possible, leaving room for doubt and differences of opinion. The teacher's role as adjudicator and referee is crucial here, with some difficult decisions about possible guidance on human behaviour and absolute values. A better approach than questioning is to ask children to act out the emotions, attitudes and judgements which a story arouse in them. We are also concerned with the behaviour and attitudes of the people portrayed in the story:-

Which words and phrases in the story tell us about the frame of mind of the characters? How emotionally charged is the language in which the story is told? How does it make us feel about each character and their actions?

Can we take up the story from different points of view? With whom shall we each choose to identify?

Why did our chosen character behave as he/she did? Can we understand and accept that point of view?

How do we feel about the courses of action open to the characters? How would we respond to these? Do we respond differently? What gaps in the story do we need our imaginations to fill?

What dangers did these people face? What did they fear most?

Examine the facts of the story very closely. What restrictions and limitations did the characters face? Are these familiar or unfamiliar to modern children? Can we interpret them together?

CRITERIA FOR 'VERDICTS'

Which emotions expressed by the various characters - anger, envy, malice, greed, jealousy, courage, selflessness etc. do children best recognize from their own limited experience? How do they respond to those feelings?

Did the victim, if any, deserve his fate? Would he have admitted this? Otherwise, how would he explain the situation to us? Do we find this explanation reasonable?

Describe several different ways in which this situation (a) could arise and (b) be reconciled. Encourage many possible explanations of the scene which the Narrator has described in one way only.

Which explanations - including the Narrator's - appear to be the best ways of understanding the problem?

In how many ways were the conditions, circumstances and behaviour different from anything in our own experience. How do we set about shaking off the prejudices of 1990, in order to offer sensible interpretations of our own and try to understand old-fashioned behaviour?

Was the action enjoyable, or were the events too terrible to be enjoyable? Was the story an account of people's mistakes? How does the story make you feel? Do the people in the story behave as we would today? Could the story have ended differently? Is there a good side and a bad side to the story? Was there a happy ending, or was that impossible? Is there a hero or a villain? Is this the story of great events, or of ordinary people? Which part in the story would you have liked to play? Were things different afterwards, because of these events? Did these events change our lives in any way? Does the story teach us any lessons for the future?

Acting it out: Work with a group of friends to act the different parts in any story. Speak their words, or the words which you believe they would have used and the actions they would have performed. Watch each other carefully and discover what this makes you feel about the value of **the evidence**, true of false.

JUNIOR FACTPACKS

With a wealth of primary source material Junior Factpacks offer teachers and students the chance to share History as it happened through the words and images of people living at the time. They are ideal for library and class display, for discussion and for topic work.

Specially designed for 9 - 13 year olds and based on the Senior pack of the same title, each junior pack has a new introduction, simplified versions of many of the documents in the Senior pack and new material. Most Junior Factpacks contain colour plates, black and white photographs, letters, extracts from diaries, books, newspaper articles and transcripts. Looseleaf in a clear A4 plastic protective binder.

Votes for Women	J1
Women at Work	J14
Slavery	J19
Women in World War 1	J21
World War 1 in the trenches	J22

Forthcoming

The French Revolution	J24
Romans	J20

Let's go

ICE SKATING

By Richard Arnold.

Let's Go Ice Skating is the latest book from Richard Arnold, a well known figure in the skating world. You are invited to join him in this artistic sport and are shown how to start, choose skates and equipment, and progress to taking (and passing) National Skating Association Tests.
He ensures that you learn the good, basic techniques on which all skating is founded, but has not forgotten the fun and recreational side for he is keen that learning to skate should be enjoyable.

This self-teach book is based on his experience as a professional skating coach and will be invaluable to club leaders, school teachers and organisers of bodies such as the Scouts and Guides (which include skating in their progress tests), and the Duke of Edinburgh Bronze Awards.
This book will be useful to schools wishing to introduce skating into the curriculum. It will be indispensable to the skating coach, whether amateur or professional.
It is easy to read, well illustrated with step-by-step drawings and photographs, and is a must for skating enthusiasts, beginning or experienced.

The author has had many years of skating experience on ice and on rollers. He is the author of four other skating books (including **Better Sport Skating** - speed and hockey on ice and rollers – and **Better Roller Skating** - the only guide to this sport: both available from ELM Publications at **£4.95** each) and is well known for his writing on sport.
He is a member of the British Ice Teachers Association (BITA) and the International Roller Skating Trainer Association (IRSTA). He is a member of the editorial staff and a regular contributor to **International Skater** Magazine.

CONTENTS INCLUDE

Let's Go Ice Skating
Figure and Dance Skating
The Basic Eights
Turns
Simple Dances/More Advanced Dances
Free Skating - Solo & Pairs
Outdoor Ice Skating
National Skating Association Elementary Tests
Mini Dictionary/Index

Price £5.95
160 pp.
Sewn Paperback.
Published Sept. 1987.
isbn 0 946139 26 1

FACKPACKS

With a wealth of primary source material factpacks offer teachers and students the chance to share history as it happened through the words and images of people living at the time. They are ideal for library and class display, for discussion and for topic work.

Most Factpacks contain colour plates, black and white photographs, letters, extracts from diaries, books and newspaper articles, transcripts and a detailed introduction and reading list. These are available looseleaf in a clear A4 plastic protective binder.

1st Series (Available Now):

Votes for Women	G1	Social Reform	G15
Immigration	G2	Propaganda	G16
Crimean War	G3	Childhood	G17
The Labour Party	G4	Germany	G18
Liberals and Reform	G5	Slavery	G19
Cromwell	G6	Women in World War 1	G21
Early Trade Unions	G7	World War 1 - in the trenches	G22
Chartism	G8	Poor Laws	G23
Reformers	G9	World War 1 - at Sea	G26
Battle of Britain	G10	The Russian Revolution	G28
The General Strike	G11	Anti Semitism	G29
English Civil War	G13	Women in World War II	G30
Women at Work	G14		

Forthcoming:

Romans	G20
The French Revolution	G24
The Arab/Israeli Conflict	G25
Conflict in Ireland	G27
China Since 1948	G31
The Depression	G32
The Wild West	G33
The History of Transport	G34

ELM PUBLICATIONS
12 Blackstone Road
Stukeley Meadows Industrial Estate
Huntingdon
Cambs
PE18 6EF

We also publish textbooks on the following subjects:

Managing People

Business Management

Travel and Tourism

Library and Information Studies

Languages

PEG series (Practical Exercises for Groups)
(Computer simulations - multi media packs)

Elm also specialises in educational resources for history

If you would like further details about our publications,
please write to us at the above address.